THE SoRDID

SECRETS
of LAS VEGAS

Quentin Parker, Paula Munier,
and Susan Reynolds

D0048269

247
SEEDY, SLEAZY,
AND SCANDALOUS
MYSTERIES
OF SIN CITY

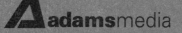

Aadamsmedia

Avon, Massachusetts

Copyright © 2011 by F+W Media, Inc.

Published by
Adams Media, a division of F+W Media, Inc.
57 Littlefield Street, Avon, MA 02322. U.S.A.
www.adamsmedia.com

ISBN 10: 1-4405-1016-4
ISBN 13: 978-1-4405-1016-8
eISBN 10: 1-4405-1194-2
eISBN 13: 978-1-4405-1194-3

Printed in the United States of America.

10 9 8 7 6 5 4 3 2 1

Library of Congress Cataloging-in-Publication Data
Parker, Quentin.
The sordid secrets of Las Vegas / Quentin Parker, Paula Munier, and Susan Reynolds.
p. cm.
ISBN-10: 1-4405-1016-4
ISBN-13: 978-1-4405-1016-8
ISBN-10: 1-4405-1194-2 (e-ISBN)
ISBN-13: 978-1-4405-1194-3 (e-ISBN)
1. Las Vegas (Nev.)—Anecdotes. 2. Las Vegas (Nev.)—Social life and customs—Anecdotes. 3.
Las Vegas (Nev.)—Biography—Anecdotes. 4. Las Vegas (Nev.)—Humor. I. Munier, Paula. II.
Reynolds, Susan (Linda Susan) III. Title.
F849.L35P375 2010
979.3'135—dc22
2010041351

This book is available at quantity discounts for bulk purchases.
For information, please call 1-800-289-0963.

DEDICATION

To my favorite two gonzo journalists: Hunter S. Thompson
and Ben Malisow.
—Quentin Parker

For my parents, the happiest people in Vegas.
—Paula Munier

ACKNOWLDGEMENTS

Many thanks to our editors Andrea Norville and Victoria Sandbrook, our book designer Ashley Vierra, our cover designer Sylvia McArdle, and the entire Adams Media team for making this book happen.

CONTENTS

Part Two: **LUST...19**

Part Seven: ENVY...171

CHAPTER 20: LARCENY...172

CHAPTER 21: MAKING IT BIG...178

INTRODUCTION

LAS VEGAS: ALL THE SINS AT ONCE

In your hometown, can you satisfy your itch for greed and gamble at the grocery store? We're not talking about scratch-off games for the so-called "education lottery." We're talking pulling slot handles or playing a few hands of video poker. Hell, no! But you can in Las Vegas. In Las Vegas, the seven deadly sins are as omnipresent as glory holes in the bus station bathroom. And greed's just the first of them. . . .

As for hometown lust, can you go to topless pool parties without worrying about police intervention or scarring the neighbors' kids for life? 'Cause you can in Vegas. Pair lust with greed and you've got the crowning glories of Sin City.

You can probably find plenty of ways to sate your gluttony fix—even in *your* hometown—but it's unlikely you've got a local hookah bar or the chance to buy a bottle of cut-rate bourbon at 5 A.M. on Sunday morning.

As for sloth: in Sin City, sloth is taken to a whole new level. Don't believe us? Do you have legions of the homeless living in your town's storm drains? Didn't think so.

If lust and greed are the queen and king of Sin City's trangressions, then wrath is this couple's crack baby, and it's crawling around everywhere! Mobsters? Check. Murderers? Check. Visits from the 9/11 hijackers and members of the Heaven's Gate cult, prior to their explosive appearances on the public scene? Check.

You might argue that some washed-up has-been of a former starlet couldn't possibly have much pride if she is *only* attracting crowds in a place where folks go to focus on other things (like greed and lust), but you'd be wrong. Even the failures in Las Vegas have a certain *je ne sais quoi*. So there. Who's famous from *your* hometown? Huh?

And finally, there's envy. Sure, you've got envy back home. You know . . . That asshole gets a promotion, and you get squat. But Las Vegas soars envy to new heights. Some believe *God himself* is so envious of Sin City that he attacked a locals' casino with a bolt of lightning!

In *The Sordid Secrets of Las Vegas*, you will learn about all of the sins that make Sin City, well, Sin City. This book is divided into seven sections, each of which focuses on one of your favorite seven deadly transgressions. It's filled with all kinds of fascinating, hysterical, and occasionally unbelievable tales that the leaders of this infamous desert community would probably prefer you did *not* know.

So, get ready to take a sin-filled armchair journey into the ugly heart of one of the world's most sinful and—let's face it—*coolest* places.

Part One

GREED

CHAPTER 1
GAMBLING

1. I'M JUST HERE TO SEE MOM. REALLY.

Only 5 percent of the people who come to Las Vegas say they come to gamble. Yet 87 percent of the people who come to Las Vegas end up gambling while they are here. That's how pervasive the betting culture is in Sin City.

And yet deluded tourists keep on coming. According to the latest annual Visitor Profile Study:

- ♣ 40 percent of visitors say they come to Las Vegas for vacation.
- ♣ 15 percent of visitors say they come to Las Vegas to visit friends and/or family.
- ♣ 9 percent of visitors say they come to Las Vegas for conventions, conferences, and/or business-related purposes.

Note: *GLS Research conducts on-the-Strip interviews with some 3,600 visitors a year to compile the data for the study, at the behest of the Las Vegas Conventions and Visitors Authority.*

2. FIVE BEN FRANKLINS

All those people who don't come to Vegas to gamble but *do* actually gamble while they are here admit to an average "gambling budget" of $500.

3. GODAWFUL GLITTER GULCH

Glitter Gulch—a.k.a. downtown Las Vegas—is to the Strip as a two-dollar whore is to a high-priced call girl. Both give you, roughly (perhaps *very* roughly, if you're into that sort of thing) the same experience, but one does it with class while the other . . . well, the other leaves you feeling like you've been with a two-dollar hooker.

Unlike the glitzy Strip, downtown evokes images of Vegas past. You know, mouth-breathers from God-knows-where and buffets that are breeding grounds for *E. coli*.

Sure, some of the downtown properties make an effort to look spiffy: Fitzgeralds, the Golden Nugget, umm . . . We're stumped. Others look like a refuge for Fellini film extras: The Western, the El Cortez, the Golden Gate . . . and, well, pretty much all the rest of them.

Some will claim the odds downtown are preferable to the odds on the Strip, but who cares? At least you're not likely to get VD from a toilet seat in The Mirage.

4. AT LEAST IT'S CHEAP . . .

Rooms at The Western Hotel and Casino may have signs reminding you not to have "guests" (i.e., hookers) in your room, but at least the place is dirt-cheap. Most nights at the Western will run you less than twenty bucks.

5. BOWLING FOR SAM'S TOWN

Chances are, if you're not from Las Vegas and you've heard of Sam's Town, it's because you're a fan of Las Vegas–based band, The Killers. The group named its sophomore effort after the locals' casino of the same name.

Sam's Town, opened in 1979, was among the first of Sin City's locals' casinos. Unlike their topless, teasing, tantalizing Strip cousins, locals' casinos are as bland and wholesome as places that offer gambling and free boilermakers for players can be.

Like other locals' places, Sam's Town is far from both the Strip and Glitter Gulch. You'll find it way out on Boulder Highway, near the place where multilane streets dwindle to tiny ribbons of asphalt before being gobbled up by the desert.

GENTLEMEN, START YOUR ENGINES

Sam's Town may not offer much excitement, but it does sponsor a NASCAR race, the Sam's Town 300. Recent winners have included Kevin Harvick, Greg Biffle, and Jeff Burton.

Sure, you can stay there if you're a tourist, and the rates are probably better than what you'll find anywhere on the Strip, but Sam's Town does not offer the "what happens in Vegas" sort of experience most people come to town seeking. Instead you'll find the same dreary bowling alleys, movie theaters, and crappy buffets you'd find back home.

6. THE LOCALS' CHOICE: THE STATION CASINOS

Lo, how the mighty have fallen. Maybe it finally dawned on people that no city, even Las Vegas, needs almost twenty properties catering principally to locals.

Palace Station opened in 1976. At the time, it was a pretty revolutionary concept: Create a casino, with all the (literal) bells and whistles, but target it to locals. The just-off-the-Strip property was a huge success, and founder Frank Fertitta, Jr. looked like a genius. The company's stock went public in 1993.

Fast forward about fifteen years. Station Casinos was in the hands of Fertitta's sons and had grown quite large through a combination of building new properties in outlying parts of Sin City, taking over existing properties, or managing properties it didn't own. Maybe it was too damn big.

The company's stock was removed from the NYSE in 2007, and in 2009, Station Casinos filed Chapter 11, claiming to be more than a *billion* dollars in debt. A little less than a month later, Fertitta the elder died from heart complications. Now he is free to roll about in his grave as the company he founded slowly dies.

> ❝ JUST BECAUSE WE HAVE A LOUSY CORPORATE CAPITAL STRUCTURE DOESN'T MEAN WE STOP RUNNING OUR PROPERTIES. ❞
>
> —Kevin Kelley, *chief operating officer*

7. SCREW TRIPLE COUPON DAYS: LET'S GO GAMBLING!

What's on your grocery list? Eggs (check), milk (check), bread (check), Double Diamond Slots (check). Yes. In Las Vegas, supermarkets aren't just for picking up pot roast. They're also dens of (gambling) iniquity. Near the front entrance/exit of your average grocery or department store, you will find rows of slot and video poker machines.

Why, you may ask yourself, does a grocery store need slot machines when the city of Las Vegas is crawling with zillions of more appropriate gambling spots? Because (and here is one of Sin City's most closely guarded secrets) Las Vegas is *not* inhabited by Earthlings.

No, seriously. Las Vegas was founded by Mormons. Some of whom believe aliens left golden plates for Jesus or something like that, right? Oh, and didn't Joseph Smith lose those plates, like, twice? However it started, from the get–go, Las Vegas was designed to appeal to folks who are *not like you and me*.

The folks in Iowa know this because they're *Earthlings* (albeit, mostly boring Earthlings).

    ALLOWING TACKY, BLINKING, BEEPING GAMBLING MACHINES FREE REIGN IN IOWA RETAIL ESTABLISHMENTS MAKES FOR A DECIDEDLY UN-IOWAN ATMOSPHERE. LAS VEGAS IS WHERE YOU EXPECT TO FIND SLOT MACHINES IN THE SUPERMARKET, NOT AMES, DAVENPORT OR WATERLOO.

—Editorial, *Iowa State Daily*

8. CASINO ROYALE

The Strip is running out of places that cater to low rollers, but there is one property—smack dab in the heart of Las Vegas Boulevard—that still wants your money. Yes, even yours, you cheap bastard.

The Casino Royale regularly features $3 minimum bets at its blackjack tables. In addition, rooms are cheap. In July 2010, a weekend night in the Casino Royale cost $79. By contrast, rooms started at $209 in next door's Venetian.

That's right. This little podunk place is next door to the Venetian and across the street from the Mirage, two of the Strip's high-priced, high-roller paradises.

Luckily for you, Casino Royale is a place you can stay on the cheap in Sin City without sacrificing location. You can come off like a high roller, and no one will ever know otherwise.

9. GRAND THEFT

The Casino Royale more than just a cheap spot on the Strip: it's also a video game star! As the "Royal Casino," Casino Royale makes an appearance in *Grand Theft Auto: San Andreas*.

10. THE SAHARA

The Sahara, which anchors the north end of the Strip, is considered the last "vintage" Las Vegas casino. It opened in 1952 and was featured in the Rat Pack classic, *Ocean's 11*. By Sin City standards, this qualifies the casino resort as a true historical landmark.

Nontheless, the Sahara looks pretty shabby compared to showplaces like Wynn, the MGM Grand, and the Venetian, which inhabits the spot once held by the quintessential Rat Pack–era casino, the Sands.

In 2006, reports surfaced that the Sahara was for sale or even on the chopping block. It's not just "age" that's going against the Sahara; it's at the "ass end" of the Strip, the last bastion of respectability (not counting the Stratosphere) before one arrives at the anti-Strip, a portion of Las Vegas Boulevard filled with nudie bars, hourly motels, pawn shops and . . . uh . . . wedding chapels!?

DINO REIGNS

In 1960's *Ocean's 11*, Dean Martin's character is shown at the Sahara performing "Ain't That a Kick in the Head," a risque song—at the time, anyway.

Entrepreneur Sam Nazarian bought the Sahara in 2007, but the future of the Sahara is still not certain. Will it be expanded? Torn down and replaced? At this point, very few really care.

11. DRINKING AND GAMBLING

Bars. They're not just for breakfast anymore! At least in Las Vegas they're not. When you belly up to a Sin City watering hole, you'll find a video poker machine in front of you, just waiting for you to get sloshed enough to throw quarters into them the way you shovel peanuts into your gullet. It's not real money as long as you're drinking, right?

MALL RATS

If you want to focus on drinking—not gambling—then strip mall bars are the places for you. You are encouraged to gamble but don't have to, and the price of drinks will be a fraction of what you'll pay at fancy places like the Palazzo's LAVO.

Now, we're not talking about the kind of high-class bars you find in Strip casinos, mind you. We're talking places kept as dark as permanent midnight in order to make sure you can't see how disgustingly filthy they are. But you're not there to play Martha Stewart, are you? Hell, no! You're there to get ripped and win some money!

12. YOU ARE NOW CLEARED FOR GAMBLING

You can tell a lot about a city from its airport. Detroit's, for example, has low ceilings and a floor that looks permanently unclean. It's the kind of place you want to escape *from*, and God help you if it's your final destination. Atlanta's airport is a buzzing hive of confusing activity, with a regular population that outstrips the entire state of Delaware.

Las Vegas's McCarran International Airport has "celebrities" (i.e., one-hit wonders and folks who once appeared in sitcoms) on the loudspeakers, telling you to keep up with your luggage. Every surface seems to gleam. And, of course, there's gambling.

After all, why wait for the casinos? Las Vegas is happy to take your money from the moment you hit the tarmac. Sure, the odds on these slot machines are purported to be deplorable, but you're in Vegas, right? You wouldn't have come if you didn't want to throw your money away.

So, before you go to the bar for overpriced drinks, shop at the stores for overpriced souvenirs, and get on the phone to book an overpriced "escort," stop and savor your very first experience with Las Vegas's principal industry. You may not even need to leave the airport at all.

WHO NEEDS DISNEY?

A monorail already connects several casinos in Las Vegas. As this book went to press, the Las Vegas Monorail Company was in the planning stages of an expansion that will reach McCarran Airport. You may never have to go outside during your Sin City stay!

13. BETTING ON *EVERYTHING*

When you watch sports with your buddies and you say things like, "I'll bet you that asshole will miss this next field goal," you get bragging rights if you're right. Well, one of the latest things to hit Sin City is a device that will allow you to win *money* instead of measly bragging rights.

Sports books—the places where you can bet on sporting events—are not traditionally big money earners in Vegas. Gambling as a whole racks up some $10 billion, but sports books only take in about $125 million.

In 2009, a handful of casinos with sports books—the Venetian, the Palazzo, M—introduced the eDeck. Looking like bulky iPhones, eDecks are portable devices folks can use to gamble on just about anything sports-related.

Players give money to the sports book, which is transformed into electronic credits. Then, as gamblers play slots or squeeze the plump behinds of cocktail waitresses, they also can bet on, say, the likelihood that the next batter will hit a home run. As if Las Vegas needed to add another addiction to their offerings!

> 66 THIS IS SOMETHING WE'LL PROBABLY HAVE IN OUR SPORTS BOOKS
> FOR A LONG, LONG TIME. 99
>
> —Mark Goldman, Venetian sports book director

14. THE WORLD SERIES OF POKER

Whoever decided that poker could be a spectator sport was probably laughed out of the office. But, as we all know, he (and it must have been a "he") got the last laugh. No "poker event" has more clout and cajones than the World Series of Poker.

The competition began in 1970 when Benny Binion invited some world-class players to his Glitter Gulch property, Binion's Horseshoe. The event grew slowly. It wasn't until 1982 that the World Series of Poker attracted more than fifty participants. By contrast, nearly *9,000* participated in the 2006 Main Event, the series's, uh, main event.

> 66 MANY USE STARES, CRYPTIC BETS, AND CONVERSATION TO WIN. 99
>
> —Oskar Garcia, poker analyst, Associated Press

Since 1972, the Main Event (yes, it's always capitalized) has been a $10,000 buy-in no-limit Texas Hold 'Em tournament. The winner gets a snazzy bracelet . . . and millions of dollars ($8.94 million in 2010).

Since 2005, the World Series of Poker has been held at the Rio, a Harrah's-owned resort off the Las Vegas Strip. Bracelet winners have included folks who have "real" jobs, such as actress Jennifer Tilly and Danish soccer player Jan Vang Sorensen.

15. NOW YOU SEE THE CASINO, NOW YOU DON'T . . . .

The most valuable properties in Las Vegas are the ones zoned for gambling. And the landowners at risk of losing that zoning will do anything to keep it. Here's the rub: to hold onto your gambling zoning designation, you have to provide gambling in a public facility at least one day every twenty-four months. For those entrepreneurs in the process of planning and building casinos, two years is often not enough time to open a swell wagering establishment.

TRACKING THE GHOST CASINOS

If you'd like to see the sun set on your money and the Trailer Station you lose it in at the same time, check the blog *www.VegasHappensHere.com*. You'll find updates from the Gaming Control Board listing the times and places of Trailer stations as they appear—and disappear.

So to keep their cherished gambling zoning designation, they throw up ghost casinos in manufactured homes. These so-called "Trailer Stations" appear on lots all over the city, whenever the need arises. Typically stripped down spaces bearing little resemblance to anything you'd see on the Strip, Trailer Stations are equipped by law with portable toilets and wheelchair-accessible entrances—and the obligatory slot machines.

There's no promotion and so few people even know they exist, much less that they are open for business. No one even has to gamble—as long as the pubic *could* gamble in a Trailer Station, that's good enough.

Here today, gone tomorrow . . . until the next time.

Just like your money.

CHAPTER 2

LAND GRUBBING

16. IF YOU BUILD IT IN VEGAS, YOU'RE SCREWED

The reinvention of Las Vegas may be punctuated by dramatic implosions, but it's the ongoing *erection* of new casinos, commercial buildings, and homes that keeps the City of Sin shiny and new. Sure, the city has seen booms and busts in inevitable cycles since the turn of the twentieth century, but this latest *fin de siecle* boom seemed one that would last forever. The Strip underwent an amazing revitalization, from one end to the other—and the blooming suburbs stretched far into the desert.

> **HAMMERED**
>
> Half of the people collecting unemployment in the state of Nevada work in the construction industry, according to Steve Holloway, executive vice president of the local chapter of Associated General Contractors.

Then the Great Recession stopped the local construction boom of the 1980s and 1990s cold—and suddenly the landscape was littered with unfinished, empty, and abandoned properties. Housing prices dropped a whopping 58 percent. Foreclosure rates soared—to more than triple that of the rest of the national average. Construction employment, which had doubled during the previous decade, plunged.

Bad news for locals—but good news for all you new homebuyers and tourists.

Wherever you are.

17. MISTAKE WITH A LAKE: THE LAKE LAS VEGAS DEBACLE

It seemed like a good idea at the time. Spend tens of millions of dollars to create a lake in the middle of the desert. Add some Jack Nicklaus–designed golf courses, a Ritz-Carlton, sprinkle in some six-figure to multimillion-dollar homes, and . . . No. On second thought, this *never* seemed like a good idea. A Ritz-Carlton in the middle of the desert!?

Lake Las Vegas now sits like an unwatered plant, some twenty miles from Vegas. It's still beautiful, but it is slowly wilting away. Some folks still live in their multimillion-dollar homes, hoping happy days will come again, as they look over the browning greens of closed-down Jack Nicklaus–designed courses. But they don't have a chance.

> "THE HOTEL IS CLOSED. THE GOLF COURSES ARE CLOSED. WHAT ARE OWNERS GETTING FOR THEIR (HOMEOWNER ASSOCIATION) DUES?
> —Dennis Smith, president, Home Builders Research

It's not like there weren't any signs of failure. An actor named J. Carlton Adair first tried to develop Lake Las Vegas forty years ago and went bankrupt by 1972. Another developer tried—and failed—before Transcontinental Corporation took over and began to find some success.

Then—screech, bang, crash—the recession hit, and Lake Las Vegas found itself underwater.

18. A YUCCA PLACE TO HIDE NUCLEAR WASTE

Yucca Mountain, about 100 miles from Las Vegas, was for two decades the proposed site for a very special landfill that would have been chock full o' the basically-eternally-lasting waste from the nation's nuclear plants. Over $10 billion (from taxpayers) was spent to get the site ready.

As a "gift" to Sen. Majority Leader Harry Reid, the Obama administration took Yucca Mountain off the nuclear table for good in 2010 due to outcries from . . . well, from pretty much everybody. Now, a new "blue ribbon task force" has been formed, and it is not expected to come up with any new nuclear waste solutions for at least two years.

Why was everyone so upset? Nuclear waste has to go *somewhere*. Dang. Don't be such NIMBY's (Not In My Back Yard)! It's not like it's . . . nuclear waste or something. Oh, wait, yeah . . . that's *exactly* what it was.

> **"**OUR QUALITY ASSURANCE REQUIREMENTS WERE NOT MET . . . WE FIND IT BEST TO JUST REPLACE THIS WORK.**"**
>
> —Assistant Secretary of the Interior, Paul Golan

19. THE BOOM . . . AND THE BUST

Desert city or not, Las Vegas spent much of the latter half of the 2000s underwater. Existing home prices shot up to an average of $285,000 in 2006. By 2010, the average was $120,000. Beginning in 2007, Sin City led the nation in home foreclosures.

> **VEGAS WON'T QUIT**
>
> Most cities would look at the global recession and say, "Damn it. It's over." But not Vegas! With plenty of desert land left to fill and a history that has given locals plenty of reason to believe that Sin City always bounces back, Las Vegas continues to build homes . . . thousands of them.

Las Vegas's population grew from around 1.5 million in the mid-1990s to around 2 million in the 2000s. Ironically, some of the boom was based on folks leaving the high-priced California housing market to settle in a place with reasonable home prices.

The gamble didn't pay off for many of these buyers. Thanks to the same cagey lending practices that led to a national recession, Las Vegas builders were putting up houses as fast as little old ladies pull nickel slot handles. Then . . . oops! Enter recession, and those expensive houses were worth a fraction of their purchase cost. Folks defaulted on their loans, etc. The housing boom became a bust.

20. CONSTRUCTION WORKER DEATHS

Las Vegas to construction workers: Drop dead.

Sin City doesn't want you to know that its rapid growth came at the cost of a dozen lives during the 2000 boom years. Still, the *Las Vegas Sun* won the 2009 Pulitzer Prize for public service reporting for a series of articles about construction-worker deaths.

> IN THE SHADOWS OF THE CRANES, STEEL, AND CONCRETE UPON WHICH LAS VEGAS HAS PINNED ITS ADDICTION TO GROWTH, A BODY COUNT HAS EMERGED.
>
> —Alexandra Berzon, *Las Vegas Sun*

Overtime didn't exist in the Las Vegas construction business until the 1990s. Up until then, folks worked eight hours and left. With the construction of Mandalay Bay, however, that changed. At the same time, contracting firms and safety regulators began jerking one another off to their mutual satisfaction but to the detriment of worker safety. When these two worlds collided, a worker died about once every six weeks.

One incident brought special attention to the situation. After *six* deaths related to MGM's CityCenter project, workers walked off the job in June 2008.

21. COSMOPOLITAN OF LAS VEGAS

Have you ever seen a white elephant being built? Would you like to? Great! Just head for the Las Vegas Strip and check out the Cosmopolitan of Las Vegas.

The Cosmopolitan hasn't attracted as much notice as its neighbor, CityCenter. Still, its original developer declared bankruptcy during the property's construction, and the original plans had nutty ideas, such as a plan to put the casino on the second floor. *The second floor!?* The casino goes on the *ground floor*, dumbass, so that passersby will be sucked in.

> **IT'S STILL BIG, BUT IT'S NOT 15 MINUTES IN TERMS OF GETTING AROUND THE CASINO.**
>
> —John Unwin, Cosmopolitan CEO

Deutsche Bank bought the property and continued to build it ... with the casino on the ground floor where it belongs. But the place still has some marketing trouble. Its major "selling point" is that it is smaller than neighboring casinos so, you know, people don't have to walk so far to get from the casino to the spa. They're marketing this place to *lazy people!* Actually, that might be a good bet.

In June 2010, the Cosmopolitan announced that it would take reservations for its December opening. Good luck, guys. You're going to need it.

22. THE LONGEST STRIKE

The hotel-casino that caused the longest successful hotel strike in American history is gone, and, most likely, many involved in the strike say, "Good riddance!"

The New Frontier closed its doors in 2007 and was imploded later that year to make way for a new Steve Wynn property. When it was still just the Frontier (no "new"), it was the site of a strike that lasted from

September 1991 to February 1998. The casino, which was making pretty good money, wanted to cut workers' wages and end their pension plans.

Folks who visited Las Vegas during the '90s grew accustomed to seeing disgruntled workers lined up on the sidewalk in front of the Frontier, signs aloft. They were as much a part of the Strip's pageantry as the volcano outside of the Mirage. When a developer bought the Frontier in 1998, the strike ended.

A LOT OF FRONTIER HISTORY

The Frontier was the site of Elvis's first (unsuccessful) Las Vegas engagement, in 1956. It was also the site of the final concert appearance of Diana Ross with the Supremes, in 1970. Howard Hughes once owned the property.

Part Two
LUST

CHAPTER 3

SHOWGIRLS

23. THOSE WERE THE DAYS

Way back in the old days of the 1950s, most Las Vegas showgirls didn't dance. As long as they were very tall, very attractive, could maneuver up and down stairs—in stilettos while wearing heavy headdresses and cumbersome feathered tails—and were willing to take off their bras, they were just what Las Vegas ordered.

> I DIDN'T INTERACT WITH THE AUDIENCE . . . I WAS JUST AN OBJECT TO BE LOOKED AT. I GAZED OVER THEIR HEADS, A BEAUTIFUL MYSTERIOUS CREATURE UP ON STAGE, BOUND IN A BEAUTIFUL COSTUME.
> —Lora Chamberland, former showgirl

Today's showgirls are more versatile and arguably more talented. Many are dancers, although old-timers kvetch that the advent of dancers led to skimpier costumes and the loss of the excessive showgirl glamour. Some modern showgirls are also magicians or acrobats.

24. THE DADDY OF ALL-AMERICAN SHOWGIRLS

Florenz "Ziggy" Ziegfeld Jr. debuted showgirls in his 1907 *Follies: Glorifying the American Girl*, which offered a series of vaudevillian acts, followed by dazzling production numbers featuring beautiful young women in glamorous, glittering costumes. The showgirls quickly became known as "Ziegfeld

Girls" and their presence separated the Follies from all other shows of the time. Busby Berkeley took it a step further by featuring showgirls in hugely spectacular musical numbers in his 1930s Hollywood films.

VIVE LA PARIS

European shows like the *Lido de Paris* had long had their own showgirl tradition, but it wasn't until French revues like the *Folies Bergère* and the *Lido* were staged in Las Vegas in the 1960s that the showgirls became famous not only in Vegas, but worldwide. *Folies Bergère* is still running at the Tropicana, and is considered by many to be one of the most popular and best Las Vegas shows with some 40,000 people filling the seats each month.

> **THERE'S ALWAYS SOMEONE YOUNGER AND HUNGRIER COMING DOWN THE STAIRS AFTER YOU.**
> —Cristal Connors, Gina Gershon's character in the movie *Showgirls*

25. FRENCH WOMEN DON'T WEAR BRAS

Minsky's Follies, which premiered in 1957 at the Dunes, was the first Las Vegas showgirl act that also included topless dancers. Some disagree, citing their opinion that the topless dancers at the Minsky show were performing more of a burlesque act than a showgirl act. Experts on the industry say modern topless shows date back to 1958, when topless dancers from the Lido de Paris Troupe at the Stardust added sexy spice to the show.

TINY DANCERS

In some smaller shows, showgirls will also dance, but in larger stage productions, there is usually a separation between showgirls and dancers. Showgirls are typically closer to 6 feet tall and statuesque, and when you add ten to thirty pound costumes, elaborate ten- to twenty-pound headdresses, and stiletto-heeled shoes, they appear larger than life. Dancers have the leeway to be shorter and are typically more lithe and light on their feet. Showgirls are often bare breasted; dancers may wear skimpier costumes, but typically cover their breasts.

26. EYES ON THE PRIZE(S)

In an interview, Paula Allen, a *Jubilee!* dancer, revealed that audiences often squirm when topless dancers first appear on the stage. "Sometimes people in the audience are embarrassed during the first act, which features all fifty nude dancers. They are afraid to make eye contact with the dancers, and they look all around. But by the second number they're used to it, and by the end of the show the nudity is no big deal. It's just Vegas."

27. CELEBRITY SNAPPER

There's nothing like nostalgia to make cities like Las Vegas look dreamy. Over three decades, beginning in the early '70s, Robert Scott Hooper was one of the few professional photographers who regularly snapped showgirls, burlesque stars, glamour girls, musicians, magicians, and performers, as well as iconic Las Vegas happenings and scenery. From 1968 to 1984, a gorgeous Hooper Cover Girl decorated the front page of each of some 832 editions of the *Vegas Visitor*, which, no surprise to us, had become an international entertainment publication. Hooper had backstage access that is rarely permitted these days, and many of his photographs were never published. Now, thanks to *www.vegasretro.com*, you can see the historic pictures and purchase any that capture your fancy.

28. THE LAST AUTHENTIC SHOWGIRL REVUE

When it comes to Las Vegas shows, *Jubilee!* at Bally's has been a Las Vegas staple since 1981, seen by more than nine million people since its debut. Produced by legendary topless show producer Donn Arden, *Jubilee!* is a lavish stage spectacular, featuring more than 100 performers, including fifty topless dancers. Some say it's the last authentic showgirl revue in Las Vegas, and, many agree, as the *Las Vegas Review-Journal* has picked it for "best showgirls" every year since 2000. It opens with a $3 million number and closes with the infamous Red Feather Fan number. Calling Gypsy!

SHOW STOPPERS

Jubilee! loves old-style excess, like three thousand gallons of water spilling from an exact replica of the *Titanic*; Samson and Delilah performing an erotic ballet clad only in g-strings; showgirls floating above the audience on platforms; and a parade of showgirls, many wearing headdresses that have to be supported by scaffolds as wide as their arm spans—and those tall beauties have very long arm spans!

> I LOVE SHOWGIRLS. THEY ARE THE LIVING, BREATHING EMBODIMENT OF EVERYTHING LAS VEGAS. I THINK THEY GET A BAD RAP.
>
> —Oscar Goodman, mayor of Las Vegas

29. BACKSTAGE SECRETS

If you're hot to peek behind the scenes, *Jubilee!* offers a walking backstage tour three days a week for anyone over the age of thirteen (just in case you stumble upon seminaked showgirls). Some tidbits from the tour:

♣ Giant elevators can whisk 100,000 pounds of sets up to the stage in seconds.

♣ Cramped dressing rooms are two stories below the stage, and, yes, you do get to peek inside.

♣ Stairs on the stage are 12 inches, twice the height of normal stairs, and the performers have to navigate them in stilettos.

30. WEARING NOTHING WEIGHS A LOT

Those outfits may be skimpy, but they can be heavy, in weight, in appearance, and in cost. Consider these facts:

♣ *Jubilee!* features more than 1,000 smashing Bob Mackie and Pete Menefee costumes.

♣ The costumes require 8,000 miles of sequins.

♣ The rhinestones used on the costumes are silver-plated Swarovski crystals.

66 CHER HAD SUCH AN UNBELIEVABLE BODY . . . SHE COULD WEAR ANYTHING. SHE WAS LIKE A BIG BARBIE DOLL. 99

—Bob Mackie, legendary costume designer

31. SWEATING WITH PASTIES

Upkeep of all those showgirl and dancer costumes is also massive, for example:

- ♣ Dancers go through 1,500 pairs of tights a year.
- ♣ Dancers change costumes as many as eleven times during a show.
- ♣ Huge headdresses, some 3 feet wide, are suspended above on ropes and lowered onto the dancers' heads.
- ♣ The costumes are so elaborate they can only be washed once a week. Luckily, each showgirl has her own costumes.

STICKER PRICE SHOCKER

The majority of *Jubilee!* dancers have second jobs and make less than dancers in other big shows on the Strip, most of whom have base salaries of at least $1,000 to $1,400 a week.

32. YOU CAN BE A SHOWGIRL TOO!

If you're harboring an inner showgirl itching to come out or if you want to surprise your lovely wife or girlfriend (or favorite gay, cross dresser, or transvestite), you can buy a custom-fitted showgirl costume at Showgirl Costumes stores in Las Vegas or online via *www.showgirlcostumes.com*. Showgirl Costumes has been a supplier to many Las Vegas productions since 1990. Each costume is handmade to fit your measurements, signed by the designer, and dated to assure authenticity. If you're hot to have one while you're in Vegas, they'll deliver it right to your hotel room. They also ship to Canada, Scotland, Ireland, London, Paris, Rio, and Bermuda . . . obviously these locations have a lot of aspiring showgirls. Just for fun, here's a taste of what's available:

♣ Hollywood: Twenty-two prime quality 2-foot ostrich plumes and 12 yards of four-ply ostrich boas; two-piece rhinestone-trimmed bra and G-String, trimmed in genuine crystals; rhinestone choker; feather and rhinestone headpiece; and gloves: $2,025; plus $600 for the headpiece and $675 for a deluxe fantail.

♣ Wedding Showgirl: Twelve prime quality 2-foot ostrich plumes and 6 yards of four-ply ostrich boa; bra, top and briefs trimmed with Austrian crystals; rhinestone bra; sequin g-string; feather headpiece on full skull cap; feather trimmed sarong; gloves; arm boa and beads: $1,200; plus boa-tail fanny pack: $375, or a super-deluxe fantail: $675, and a dancing fan: $250.

♣ Accoutrements: A real crystal full-rhinestone bra built on pushup foundation: $800 (for Aurora Borealis stones instead of clear add $100); rhinestone g-strings and garters: $300; handcrafted rhinestone "glitz" choker with five strands dropping to your navel: $350.

> **I ALWAYS TRY TO BALANCE THE LIGHT WITH THE HEAVY—A FEW TEARS OF HUMAN SPIRIT IN WITH THE SEQUINS AND THE FRINGES.**
> —Bette Midler

33. NUDIE CUTIES

If you're a woman, or a gay male, hankering for a nudie show of your own, of course you'll find one in Vegas. *The American Storm*, for one, offers a sexy male revue that features hunks, some of who have graced the covers of *Playgirl* and *Muscle & Fitness* magazine.

CHAPTER 4

PROSTITUTION AND ADULTERY

34. PAHRUMP PROSTITUTION

No other state of the union—not even New Jersey!—has legalized and government-regulated prostitution. Nope. The classy Silver State is the only place where you can pay to bust a nut without having to worry about undercover cops. God bless the State of Nevada!

But you can't get no satisfaction in Las Vegas . . . at least, not legally. In fact, legalized prostitution is only available in eight of Nevada's seventeen counties. Some—if you can believe this—*could* have hoes for hire but think it's sinful or something and therefore don't allow it. Ha! Ha! Ha!

So, if you're horny in Vegas—and who isn't—and want to enjoy the experience of paying total strangers for meaningless sex, then you've got to hump it over to Nye County, about sixty miles away.

Take Highway 160. Once in Pahrump, look for Manse Road. Just before the road turns to dust, you can set your heart (or other body parts) for lust. Naughty neighbors Sheri's Ranch and the Chicken Ranch await your intimate bodily fluids (and your money, of course).

35. PAHRUMP OR BUST

" THERE'S NO PROSTITUTION IN LAS VEGAS. EVERYBODY KNOWS THAT FOR THAT SORT OF THING, YOU HAVE TO GO TO PAHRUMP! "
—Megan Edwards, Living-las-vegas.com blogger

36. SHERI'S RANCH

Most Nevada brothels have a hook (a hook, mind you, not a hooker). Sheri's is that it's an upscale resort, complete with swimming pool, upscale rooms, tennis courts, and women who will have sex with you for money.

You're probably asking yourself, "Why does a legal brothel need a hook?" Or, maybe you're asking yourself, "Why can I only get laid when I pay women for it?" We can't help you with the latter question, and . . . well, now that we think about it, we can't really answer the former either. After all, isn't the main attraction of *any* brothel the women on the menu?

And, yes. That's what brothels call their services. Look on Sheri's menu, for example, and you will find the following fare available: Vibrator Party, Two Woman Show, Hot French Oil Massage, and Drag Party, among others. What you won't find is prices.

> ANN LANDERS SAID THAT YOU ARE ADDICTED TO SEX IF YOU HAVE SEX MORE THAN THREE TIMES A DAY, AND THAT YOU SHOULD SEEK PROFESSIONAL HELP. I HAVE NEWS FOR ANN LANDERS: THE ONLY WAY I AM GOING TO GET SEX THREE TIMES A DAY IS IF I SEEK PROFESSIONAL HELP.
>
> —Jay Leno

All of the Ladies (you will not find the words "hooker," "ho," or "prostitute" on any of Sheri's material) are independent contractors. What they charge is up to them.

37. ONLY IN NEVADA

Most folks running for office would do all they could to avoid association with a brothel, but in Las Vegas, legal brothels often contribute to local candidates. For example, Sheri's Ranch (or at least its parent company), gave $500 to Nye County district attorney candidate Ron Kent in the spring of 2010.

38. CHICKEN RANCH

All brothels that refer to themselves as "ranches" have the original Chicken Ranch to, uh, thank, we guess. That (in)famous Texas brothel, which closed in 1973, got its name because it used to take chickens in lieu of cash payment, during the Great Depression.

> **WHOREHOUSE HISTORY**
>
> The Nevada Chicken Ranch contains lots of memorabilia from the Texas Chicken Ranch. That ranch is the one on which the play and the movie *The Best Little Whorehouse in Texas* is based.

The legal, almost-in-Vegas version of the Chicken Ranch does not, however, take chickens or any other sort of poultry. Instead, the place has a reputation for being on the pricey end of legal brothels.

The Chicken Ranch opened in Pahrump, about sixty miles from Sin City, in 1976. At first, the place faced a lot of local opposition. Someone even burned the ranch down in 1978. Most likely, the culprits belonged to other legal, local brothels that did not welcome new competition.

> " DURING SEX I FANTASIZE THAT I'M SOMEONE ELSE. "
>
> —Richard Lewis

Like its across-the-street neighbor, Sheri's Ranch, the Chicken Ranch offers a variety of specialties on its "menu," including something called "audio delight," which allows you to "listen to different fantasies while enjoying your favorite (sexual) appetizer." No thanks. We'll just settle for the "straight lay."

39. HEIDI FLEISS'S "DIRTY LAUNDRY"

As a woman on top (ahem) of the sex industry, Heidi Fleiss (a.k.a. the Hollywood Madam) decided to create a business where the tables would be truly turned. In 2005, after her infamous bust for running a high-priced prostitution ring, she moved to Las Vegas and announced she would be opening a brothel—for women! Heidi Fleiss's Stud Farm would be *the* place for women looking for some love to rent a man for an hour or two. But, as mentioned previously in this chapter, prostitution is illegal in Las Vegas. Of course, Heidi hit some snags along the way, like when her felony conviction due to a Nevada law against male prostitutes axed her chances to peddle male ass. So, she decided to get "clean" and open the Dirty Laundry Laundromat in Pahrump, Nevada—a far stretch from a male brothel, but still practical. Even though she couldn't open her own "stud farm," she's still connected to the brothel biz. She is reportedly now engaged to Dennis Hof, the owner of Nevada's Moonlite Bunny Ranch.

> I AM OPENING UP A STUD FARM. I AM GOING TO HAVE THE SEXIEST MEN ON EARTH. WOMEN ARE GOING TO LOVE IT.
>
> —Heidi Fleiss

YOU GET WHAT YOU PAY FOR

According to *SeXis Magazine*, women, like men, *are* paying for sex. The target market for male escorts are professional women who don't have a lot of time but do have expendable incomes.

40. AIR FORCE AMY

Get that thing to full attention, soldier! Air Force Amy's just down the street, and she offers discounts for armed forces personnel.

Donice Armstrong grew up a nice little Catholic girl in Cleveland before joining the Air Force. Just before she left the armed services, however, she applied to a Nevada brothel, and she's been working at the world's oldest profession ever since.

> " MY TYPICAL DAY IS PROBABLY A LOT MORE FUN THAN YOURS. "
> —Air Force Amy

Air Force Amy, uh, came to the world's attention via the HBO documentary (later the series) *Cathouse*, which focuses on—what else—life in Nevada's legal brothels. In the summer of 2010, as the star of Ron Jeremy's film, *Lesbian Ho'Down at the Bunnyranch*, Air Force Amy made the hearts and tingly body parts of men and women in Vegas skip a beat.

Air Force Amy announced that she had left the Carson City area to move "over the hump" to Pahrump. You now can find her at Sheri's Ranch (see #36), and, yes, she still offers those armed service personnel discounts. Hell, we're going to go enlist *right now*.

41. WEAR A CONDOM—IT'S THE LAW!

In Nevada, wearing a condom when you have sex isn't just advised: it's mandatory. In the more than two dozen legal brothels where some 300 prostitutes entertain clients, condoms have been required for all acts of oral sex and sexual intercourse since 1988.

Commercial sex workers have been tested for sexually transmitted diseases (STDs) since 1986—on a weekly basis for gonorrhea and Chlamydia trachomatis, and on a monthly basis for HIV and syphilis. Compliance rates within the brothels are high as evidenced by the relatively low rates of STDs.

> CONDOMS AREN'T COMPLETELY SAFE. A FRIEND OF MINE WAS
> WEARING ONE AND GOT HIT BY A BUS.
>
> —Bob Rubin

Ironically, surveys of legal prostitutes reveal that while they may use condoms religiously at work, they rarely use them when having sex in their off-hours.

42. TWO CONDOMS *ARE* BETTER THAN ONE

Compliance with Nevada's laws requiring condom use at brothels is not only good, it's great. A study of the legal prostitutes in these heavily regulated, licensed brothels has shown that many ensure their safety as well as that of their customers by using two condoms to prevent breakage. According to study participants, the reasons sex workers insist on the wearing of two condoms rather than one include:

- ♣ Prior experiences with breakage
- ♣ Customers with particularly big penises
- ♣ Customers with penile sores or marks
- ♣ Thin condoms
- ♣ Requests from customers

The mandatory use of condoms during every act of commercial sex and the frequent use of two condoms during most acts of commercial sex has resulted in lower rates of sexually transmitted diseases, including HIV, among Nevada legal prostitutes than among female prostitutes in other states. (Source: *American Journal of Public Health*)

43. THE JOHN ENSIGN SEX SCANDAL

Nevada's *other* Senator is a Pentecostal. Who knew? He's allegedly guilty of having extramarital affairs and using influence to try to hush them up. Now, that's more like Sin City!

Senator John Ensign is one of those fundamentalist conservatives who believes that no one should be allowed to do anything fun with anyone ever . . . unless of course, *he's* the one having fun.

John Ensign has served as Senator from Nevada since 2001, and he may be the only Senator on Capitol Hill who was a veterinarian prior to running for office. When he's home in Vegas, he attends a foursquare gospel church . . . when he's not (allegedly) boffing aide Cynthia Hampton, that is.

> **I DID NOT HAVE SEX WITH THAT WOMAN.**
>
> —John Ensign . . . *oops*, wait, that was Bill Clinton

In 2008, Hampton's husband got a sinecure with a Nevada political consulting firm. That same year, Ensign's parents gave the Hamptons a "gift" of $96,000. Hmm. That doesn't sound suspicious *at all*. Dude. Using your *parents* to spread around hush money? Apparently, that's what Jesus would have done. As this book went to press, Ensign was reportedly getting significant attention from the FBI and from the Senate Ethics (ha, ha) Committee.

44. VEGAS'S "CULTURE OF ADULTERY" RUINS TIGER WOODS

Oh, please. Reports that Las Vegas is to blame for Tiger Woods's fall from grace—a theory presented by newspapers around the world—beyond lame.

Sure, Tiger was surrounded by lots of beautiful women while he won—and lost—millions of dollars gambling with his pals Charles Barkley and Michael Jordan at such swank clubs as the Mansion at the MGM Grand, the Bank at the Bellagio, and the Tryst at the Wynn. All clubs as well known for their discretion as for their posh factor.

So what? Wherever Tiger goes, he's surrounded by lots of beautiful women. Las Vegas isn't alone in that. If he can't resist them, well, then that's his problem. (And apparently it's a big problem.)

Don't blame Sin City for Tiger's sins—or yours.

> **I'VE WORKED FOR SOME OF THE BEST IN THE BUSINESS AT SOME OF THE BEST PLACES BETWEEN NEW YORK AND LAS VEGAS.**
> —Rachel Uchitel, Hamptons party girl reputedly involved with Tiger Woods

CHAPTER 5

PORNOGRAPHY AND STRIPPERS

45. THAT'S (ADULT) ENTERTAINMENT!: THE AEE

Even in January, Las Vegas is pretty warm, but it gets smokin' hot once the Adult Video News Magazine's Adult Entertainment Expo (AEE) comes to town, heaping a great big dose of "sin" into Sin City.

While the event has the usual trade expo stuff—boring lectures on how to make your adult business thrive during tough economic times—it has to be the only one offering participants a chance to ride a seven foot penis, mechanical bull style.

> 66 OK, I DON'T KNOW ABOUT YOU GUYS, BUT I SAW *AVATAR*, AND ALL I WANTED TO DO WHEN I GOT TO THE MOVIE THEATER WAS FUCK SOMETHING BIG AND BLUE. 99
>
> —Kelly Madison, adult star, at the 2010 AEE, on the future of 3-D porn

Over three hundred companies peddled their wares at the 2010 AEE Expo. These included Slick Chix, "providing the very best in female oil wrestling for your entertainment," and the Blowguard, a "mouth vibrator for better, longer oral sex."

Many of the expo's events are open solely to (large) members of the trade, but some are open to the public, who can get autographs from and gain proximity to women who are way, way, *way* out of their league.

46. WELCOME TO LAS VEGAS. HERE'S YOUR PORN!

If you're traveling alone in Las Vegas, you might get lonely. But never fear! There are creepy, shifty-eyed gentlemen lined up all along Las Vegas Boulevard who are eager—really, really eager—to disseminate information about Sin City's various escort services.

Las Vegas is (in)famous for its pamphleteers, scary-looking guys who will place into the hands of all pedestrians (grandmas, grandpas, nuns, Buddhist monks in saffron robes) publications that look like poorly produced jerk-off magazines. Inside, you will find charming photos of naked escorts with charming little star-shaped white spots covering their woo woo's and ta ta's.

MOST EMBARRASSING MOMENTS

For many years, poor-man's-porn-peddling along the Strip has been ranked "The Most Embarrassing Thing about Las Vegas" by readers of the city's main newspaper, the *Las Vegas Review-Journal*. And the discarded copies of these pamphlets give Las Vegas the distinction of having piles of sexually explicit trash.

Since prostitution isn't legal in Las Vegas, the skanky young ladies in these books aren't hookers. They're *escorts*. Yes, they will escort you to your hotel and then escort you to sexual climax, but whatever you do . . . don't call them hookers because prostitution isn't (wink, wink; nudge, nudge) legal in Las Vegas.

> OBSCENITY IS WHATEVER GIVES THE JUDGE AN ERECTION.
> —Author Unknown

47. SAPPHIRE

Seventy-one thousand square feet of tits and ass. Is this heaven? No, it's Sapphire Gentlemen's Club near the Strip.

How big is the club? It's hard to say. Some websites call it the world's largest strip club. Others call it the largest strip club in Vegas. Sapphire splits this consensus down the middle and bills itself "the world's largest Las Vegas strip club." It makes the original Sapphire—in New York City— look like a postage stamp (one you'd really, really like to lick).

> BECAUSE OF THE CLUB'S MASSIVE SIZE (IT'S SERIOUSLY HUGE), YOU DON'T GET THE FEELING THAT YOU'RE IN SOME OFF-THE-BEATEN-PATH DIVE CLUB WHERE YOU MIGHT GET MUGGED AND NO ONE WOULD NOTICE.
>
> —Jamie Helmick, Vegas.com

Once inside, you'll find that Sapphire is a little bit nudie joint and a little bit nightclub. The place has ten VIP skyboxes overlooking the dance floor. It has three rooms, including one devoted to male strippers.

Because of Sapphire's size, it has more half-naked women per square foot than you'll find in the average horny teenager's wildest fantasies.

48. THE PLAYBOY CLUB

Once upon a time, the world was filled with Playboy Clubs. Founded by Hugh Hefner, the first club opened in 1960 in Chicago. The clubs were the hippest, hottest night spots in the world, and owning a Playboy Club key—which gained you entrance—was a status symbol.

By the 1980s, however, the Playboy Clubs seemed . . . well, quaint. Old-fashioned. You expected to see grannies in leotards, not hot, young, busty babes. The original club closed in 1986. The final American club closed in Lansing, Michigan in 1988, and the final international club closed its doors in 1991 in Manila.

> " THE MAJOR CIVILIZING FORCE IN THE WORLD IS NOT RELIGION. IT'S SEX. "
> —Hugh Hefner

Fast-forward a decade. Thanks in large part to the reality show, *The Girls Next Door*, Playboy is back to being hip and hot. And, without a doubt, Las Vegas is the hippest, hottest spot on planet Earth. So, it's no surprise these two sweet kids came together in 2006. That year, the Playboy Club was reborn at the Palms, the former site of the Desert Inn. Nowadays, the Bunnies don't just serve drinks. They also deal blackjack on the 52nd floor of the Palms's Fantasy Tower.

49. CRAZY HORSE 3

Maybe the third time will be a charm for this Las Vegas T&A landmark.

The original Crazy Horse Saloon on Paradise got gobbled up into Rick Rizzolo's Crazy Horse Too, on Industrial. But Rizzolo was implicated in Operation G-Sting (see #118), a bribery scandal that rocked Las Vegas and San Diego and took down a number of prominent politicians. As part of a plea bargain, Rizzolo was forced to sell his lucrative strip club. It was bought in April 2010 for $10 million by trucking company owner, Christopher Condotti.

> " WE WERE OMITTED FROM THE SETTLEMENT PROCESS INITIALLY. . . . THERE WAS NO REQUEST OF US AS TO WHAT OUR ATTITUDE OR OPINION WOULD BE AS FAR AS FUTURE LICENSING IS CONCERNED. "
> —Las Vegas Mayor Oscar Goodman

In 2009, Crazy Horse 3 opened on Russell Road. But here's where it gets weird. This club is *not* owned by folks associated with Crazy Horse Too, and as this was being written, the owners of Crazy Horse Too and Crazy Horse 3 were negotiating over who would get to keep the name, and it was possible that the "new, improved" Crazy Horse Too would not be given a liquor license.

This is too complicated. Just go look at some tits and ass.

50. CHEETAH'S

If you're a fan of *Showgirls*, one of the all-time worst films ever made—and who isn't, really—then Cheetah's will look familiar to you. It's the spot where character Nomi Malone plies her trade and learns to be a manipulative bitch par excellence.

> 66 IT DOESN'T SUCK. 99
>
> —Nomi Malone's most repeated line in *Showgirls*

It's also another club tainted by Operation G-Sting (see #118), the federal investigation that revealed that some strip clubs were bribing public officials. Shocking!

Oh, and it's also one of the classic tits and ass places in Sin City. Opened in 1991, Cheetah's (which sometimes uses the apostrophe and sometimes does not) has more stripper poles than some states have citizens.

The joint also features the G-Spot, a private room for lap dances. Covered with mirrors, it's the perfect place to watch yourself engaging in simulated sex with a woman who would never look at you in real life.

Cheetah's also has some aspects of a sports bar, such as giant TVs all over the place, showing various events. But who wants to look at sports when you can watch topless women slithering up and down a pole? No red-blooded American male *we* know.

51. YOU'RE NEVER TOO YOUNG FOR PORN

In Nevada, porn is a relative term. In a state where everything from gambling to prostitution and most everything in between is legal somewhere within its boundaries, the lines between right and wrong are blurred at best. To the point where the good citizens of the Battle Born State are undoubtedly confused by the morally ambiguous climate in which they live—and that confusion sometimes results in some very bad behavior.

Take Derek Henry Haase, the thirty-three-year-old Nevadan who liked to watch porn on his computer. Which made him just like millions of other guys, not all of them in Nevada. But the father of an eight-year-old girl watched his pornographic movies while his daughter was in the same room, standing behind him with a bird's eye view of the graphic sexual acts portrayed on the screen. Which means that either he was exceptionally stupid or perverted or both . . . or it was really, really good porn (not that *we* sanction the behavior).

Unfortunately for Haase, his daughter went home to her mother, his ex-wife, and demonstrated some of what she had seen at Dad's house. Her inappropriate behavior alarmed her mother, who in turn alerted the authorities.

Ultimately, Haase pled guilty to contributory neglect, and received a ninety-day suspended jail sentence and a year's probation.

52. JESUS LOVES PORN STARS

That's just one of the catchy slogans used by the XXXchurch in its campaign against pornography. The Las Vegas–based religious organization is known for its creative if controversial approach to its antiporn mission, including outreach to the sex industry and a host of events designed to spread the word against porn. The Christian group's active ministry involves:

- ♣ Passing around Bibles at adult entertainment conventions
- ♣ Selling T-shirts, books, software, and skateboard decks
- ♣ Conducting "The Porn Debate" on college campuses nationwide between porn legend Ron Jeremy and XXXchurch Pastor Craig Gross

For your own Jesus Loves Porn Stars T-shirt, check out *www.xxxchurch.com*.

> "PEOPLE THINK THEY'RE NOT AFFECTED BY THIS. BUT YOU HAVE A PORN STAR RUNNING FOR SENATE, YOU'VE GOT KIDS IN SCHOOL WEARING SHIRTS THAT SAY PORN STAR ON THEM, YOU'VE GOT THE GLAMORIZED GALS LIVING WITH HUGH HEFNER . . ."
>
> —Craig Gross, pastor of XXXchurch

CHAPTER 6

CONVENTIONS AND GATHERINGS

53. GETTIN' SOME TAIL(HOOK)

Conventions are for colleagues to share ideas, for professionals to gain continuing education experience, and for drunk, horny military dudes to grope and grab women. Just ask anyone with lactation-capable breasts who attended 1991's infamous Tailhook Association Symposium at the Las Vegas Hilton.

> **IF YOU HAVE CLOTHES THAT ARE SCANT, IF YOU HAVE A PAST THAT IS NOT PROFESSIONAL, THEN THAT'S GOING TO ADD TO THE PROBLEMS.**
>
> —Randy "Duke" Cunningham, former Republican congressman and Vietnam War veteran, on the "causes" of the Tailhook Scandal

Technically, the symposium was designed to offer naval and marine fliers a debriefing on their efforts during Operation Desert Storm. But, in fact, it became a quintessential Sin City scene of debauchery. There was only one problem. Tailhook was filled with professional servicewomen who were also war veterans. Oddly enough, they didn't like being pawed and groped like strippers with cartoon-sized fake breasts.

Ultimately, eighty-three women claimed to be victims of sexual harassment or assault. The careers of fourteen admirals and nearly three hundred servicemen were derailed by the subsequent scandal. Dang. Weren't any real strippers or Britney or Snooki available? Reportedly, they like being groped.

54. SWINGING VEGAS

Of course there are swinger's clubs in Sin City, and three of them are in the commercial district, within walking distance from each other. Each has its own attractions: thematic rooms, fantasy rooms, orgy rooms with a view, dungeons, hot tubs, unisex showers, lingerie shops, and lockers to store those pesky street clothes. In case you're worried about, um, your health, these clubs pride themselves on being "very clean." One doesn't offer a hot tub or spa for sanitary reasons, and another promises to wipe down and sanitize after each use. They don't say what they're sanitizing, but. . . . They also boast that they "do not overrun the club with single men." Charges range from free to all single women to $100 if you're a man who shows up in a cab. Don't ask us why there's an extra charge for cabbing it because we have no idea.

55. PLAYING BY THE RULES

According to the Las Vegas Swingers Club, there are "swinger lifestyle" rules that one should abide by when swinging in Vegas:

- ♣ Follow the golden rule: "No means No!"
- ♣ Singles mingle separately: Some areas are for couples and invited guests only!
- ♣ Don't offer to pay your *swingee*: Swingers are not prostitutes!
- ♣ It ain't about love, baby: Swingers are very secure in their marriages, so single men trying to complicate matters are not welcome.
- ♣ Parolees have a dress code: Don't dress like a thug.

56. THE LION'S DEN

Just in case you're in a swinging mood, here are four (literally) swinging clubs in Vegas:

- ♣ **Fantasy Swingers' Club.** Offers tours for $20, which can be applied to the cost of admission.
- ♣ **The Green Door.** This one has 18,000 square feet, including a Dungeon, and offers One-Day Teazer passes; Weekly Players' Cards; and Monthly Lifestyles Cards.
- ♣ **Red Rooster.** The granddaddy of swingers' clubs, founded in 1982, is a little off the beaten track (blushing pun intended). A homey ranch-style house that gives the feel of walking into someone's expansive basement.
- ♣ **Red Rooster 3.** A social and swingers club for couples and singles, providing a loose, relaxed atmosphere. Is there any other atmosphere suitable for swingers?

HO, HO, HO ... HO

The infamous Red Rooster celebrates all the major holidays, including a candlelight dinner for Thanksgiving, and a rollicking Christmas Party. Here's the invitation posted on their website:

Come share a great Christmas dinner with all your Rooster friends.
The Red Rooster kinky Santa will be appearing once again.
This Santa does not just cum down chimneys!

❝ SCHWING! ❞
—Austin Powers

57. FROM RAT PACK TO BRAT PACK

If you're in Vegas and hankering for a spanking, you need go no further than Shadow Lane, the Las Vegas based producer of spanking erotica and sponsor of biannual "spanking mixers." Founder Eve Howard "loves bringing spanking people together" and claims to have united countless couples for more than twenty years. Via their website (*www.shadowlane .com*) members have access to personals, chat rooms, a bulletin board, video clips, story departments, photos, spanking illustrations. If you're itching for a bitching spank, you may want to check out 2010's annual spanking mixer, which will be a Prom Night event with a *Mad Men* theme. One suspects a lot of ladies will line up to spank or be spanked by Don Draper look-a-likes; and men will likely love the idea of defrosting Betty Draper. Spanking, or what some enthusiasts call "romantic discipline" is permitted in the ballroom, as long as it's over clothing, panties, or briefs . . . bare bottom spanking is reserved for "private rooms."

And if you're shy about spanking in public, Shadow Lane offers more than 115 videos, available for private (or public) viewing, and what Howard calls "female friendly" erotica. If you're bolder, you might enjoy the annual spanking convention, where you can "road test" spanking accoutrements and find the schoolteacher paddle, twisted sister cane, or cowboy strap of your dreams.

58. SPANKER ATTIRE

The most popular costumes for spanking outings include:

Public
- ♣ Catholic schoolgirl
- ♣ Cheerleaders

- ♣ Preppie attire
- ♣ Frilly panties

Private

- ♣ Dungeon
- ♣ Full-body latex
- ♣ Leather, leather, leather
- ♣ Exposed bosom and bottom corsetry

> **BABES IN TOY LAND**
>
> Holisticwisdom.com is a website where one can seek "sensual empower-ment," and every imaginable sex toy on the planet. You can even sample erotic stories and see lists of the Top Twelve Green Sex Toys, the Worst Sex Toys, etc.

❝AFFABLE GENTLEMEN WHO DON'T DEMAND TOO MUCH OFTEN HAVE THE BEST LUCK IN GETTING A SUBMISSIVE LADY TO CROSS OVER TO THE OTHER SIDE.❞

—Eve Howard

59. FUR AND LOATHING IN LAS VEGAS

In the subculture of "geekdom," furries are human beings who identify so strongly with, well, furry animals that they don furry costumes (or ears, tails, whiskers, etc.) and show off their "animalistic characteristics" at events, including more than forty furry conventions held annually around the world—including, of course, one in Las Vegas. Ever since furries were negatively, and inaccurately, portrayed as sexual perverts in a *CSI* epi-sode (thanks to a nasty raccoon in "Fur and Loathing," season 4, episode 5), they have barred media from conventions. In 2008, Nemo Design in Portland, Oregon presented "Furry Kama Sutra," a photography/video exhibition by New York based photographer Michael Cogliantry.

Although the majority of furries are indulging innocent fantasies, furverts are a subculture within the subculture whose participants love to dress up as the animal of their choice to explore the ultimate joys of anonymous sex. You'll find them almost exclusively online.

> I ENJOY MYSELF AS A HUMAN, NORMALLY, BUT IT'S A VERY NICE THING TO JUST BE ABLE TO MAKE PEOPLE SMILE.
>
> —Ryan Vannier, twenty-five, who often dresses like a fox

60. THE FETISH AND FANTASY BALL

Dubbed the "most adult of all the adult Halloween events in Las Vegas" by *Las Vegas Weekly*; one of the top ten events in the world by the Travel Channel; and one of five events to attend before you die by *Maxim* magazine, the Fetish and Fantasy Halloween Ball is one hell of a Halloween party, famous for its "anything goes" attitude in the penultimate "anything goes" city. In 2009, a record 6,200 revelers gathered to watch erotic stage performances, fire performers, laser and light shows, aerialists, stilt walkers, freaks, monsters, and all manner of fetishers get their party on. World-class DJs had revelers bumping and grinding on two huge dance floors, while braver partygoers headed to the "audience participation" stage for a real taste of the wild side. Some revelers opted for skybox rentals at $3,500 each, giving them a bird's-eye view of the action.

> TO AVOID CAUSING ANY MAJOR SKIRMISHES OR MOBILIZATIONS OF THE 'PRUDES FOR THE ELIMINATION OF EROTIC PARTIES' (PEEP-ERS), PLEASE COVER YOUR NAUGHTY CREATIONS WHEN COMING TO AND FROM THE EVENT.
>
> —Fetish and Fantasy Ball Organizers

61. ALMOST ANYTHING GOES

Noting that "the fragile reputation of Las Vegas is at stake" (wink) and adhering to "the wisdom of our elected officials," Fetish and Fantasy ball organizers posted a dress code on their website that clearly states that *no nudity will be allowed.* Also, pasties and liquid latex are no longer acceptable, nor are rubber or other artificial genitalia. What is allowed follows:

- ♣ Costumes of any type
- ♣ Fantasy and fetish wear, such as uniforms, leather, lingerie, latex, rubber, p.v.c., lace, feathers, saran wrap, or anything else you might dream up
- ♣ Formalwear, meaning tuxes for men, gowns for ladies
- ♣ Ladies may wear sheer fabrics, and revealing outfits
- ♣ Costume weapons of any sort will not be allowed

62. NO REST ON CLOSET SUNDAYS

If you're gay and you're in Las Vegas on a Sunday then there's only one place to be: the Revolution Lounge at the Mirage. Every week Eduardo Cordova, the hippest guy in Las Vegas, presents a fun-filled evening of LGBT (lesbian, gay, bisexual, transgender) entertainment that boasts the likes of Khloe Kardashian, Lance Bass, and Janice Dickinson. From high fashion and top-rated shows to dancing and DJs, Closet Sundays is the first upscale gay-friendly ongoing event in Sin City.

Sundays aren't the only nights to boast cool LGBT events with Eduardo's name on them. Eduardo also runs the Saturday night Heaven event at Bare pool at the Mirage. Winged angels will welcome you into Heaven, where anything—and everything—heavenly can happen. Enter at your known risk.

"I LIVED IN MEXICO UNTIL I WAS EIGHTEEN. WENT TO COLLEGE IN ARIZONA, WHERE I MADE GREAT FRIENDS AND MET PEOPLE THAT CHANGED MY LIFE. I LIVED IN LA FOR A YEAR AND THEN MOVED TO LAS VEGAS TO START MY OWN BUSINESS. I LIKE LIVING IN THIS CITY FULL OF GREAT YOUNG PEOPLE AND OPPORTUNITIES. IF YOU SEE ME AROUND, SAY HELLO, I LIKE MEETING NEW PEOPLE AND MAKING NEW FRIENDS."

—Eduardo Cordova

63. A SINGLE MAN IN LAS VEGAS

Eduardo Cordova and his upscale gay parties aside, there are other go-to destinations for gays and lesbians in town:

- ♣ Krave, the Strip's only gay club, at the Planet Hollywood Resort and Casino
- ♣ Snick's Place, Las Vegas's coziest—and oldest—gay bar, think Cheers with drag queens
- ♣ Flex, known for its freewheeling booze, strippers, and games
- ♣ Badlands Saloon, festooned with stag heads and six shooters, offers country music on the jukebox and the cheapest pool game in town

LADIES' NIGHT
Many gay clubs run Ladies Nights for the lesbian community. Check out the Beer Bust on Tuesdays at Freezone or the Girlspot at Gipsy on Fridays.

CHAPTER 7

WEDDINGS AND OTHER DRUNKEN DECISIONS

64. THE PINK CADILLAC OF COMMITMENT CEREMONIES

Nevada may have a constitutional law banning same-sex marriages but that doesn't stop enterprising wedding chapels from profiting from the commitment ceremony business. At the Gay Chapel of Las Vegas, gay and lesbian couples can have the commitment ceremonies of their dreams. Options include:

♣ Go Egyptian (slave boys carry you in on a litter Cleopatra style)
♣ Fairy Tales (bring your own Prince Charming!)
♣ Gothic (in which the Grim Reaper makes an appearance)

And here's the best part: Every ceremony is broadcast live on the Internet.

> THEY ARE PRESERVING THE SANCTITY OF MARRIAGE, SO THAT
> TWO GAY MEN WHO'VE BEEN TOGETHER FOR TWENTY-FIVE
> YEARS CAN'T GET MARRIED, BUT A GUY CAN STILL GET DRUNK IN
> VEGAS AND MARRY A HOOKER AT THE ELVIS CHAPEL! THE SANC-
> TITY OF MARRIAGE IS SAVED!
>
> —Lea DeLaria

65. SO YOU THINK YOU CAN POLE DANCE

Pole dancing is an art best taught by the pros. And in Las Vegas, there is no shortage of pros to teach you the right moves. In fact, there are several schools to choose from; make sure you get your money's worth. Forget pole dancing "fitness" taught by fitness professionals. If you want to learn to do a pole dance, what you need is a pole, and a stripper who makes a living wrapping her legs around hard lengths of steel.

WRAP YOUR LEGS AROUND THIS!

The top ten sexiest pole dancing moves to master are:

- ♠ Fireman
- ♠ Butterfly Trick
- ♠ Inverted Straddle Move
- ♠ Superman
- ♠ Tail Split
- ♠ Corkscrew
- ♠ Venus Spin
- ♠ Bow and Arrow
- ♠ Blade
- ♠ Crucifix

"NOW YOU GET UP THERE AND WORK THAT POLE LIKE A RUSSIAN IMMIGRANT."

—Tina Fey as Claire Foster in *Date Night*

66. GIRLS GONE VEGAS WILD

There's a reason Las Vegas is the number one destination for bachelorette parties. Before a girl promises to forsake all others until death does she part, she needs to let loose. That's why God made bachelorette parties, and that's why *She* made Las Vegas. Forget about the anxious groom. It's the stressed-out bride who really needs one last hurrah.

And Las Vegas has everything a girl needs to blow off some steam. From manicures and pedicures to naked hunks from Thunder Down Under and Chippendales thrusting their assets in your face, there's something for every adventurous bride, including:

- ♣ Spa treatments
- ♣ Shopping
- ♣ Clubbing
- ♣ Male reviews
- ♣ Sex toy parties
- ♣ Lap dancing lessons
- ♣ Oral sex instruction

67. PASS THE PENIS FAVORS, PLEASE

The right accessories always make the difference—and bachelorette party suits are no exception. Sure, feather boas and sparkly tiaras are cute, but what really get the girls going are:

- ♣ Shot glasses
- ♣ Inflatable male dolls
- ♣ Sticky Willies
- ♣ Penis candy
- ♣ Pecker Poppers
- ♣ Penis Pops
- ♣ Pin the Macho on the Man
- ♣ Penis squirt guns

68. 'TIL DEATH (OR SOBRIETY) DO US PART

Las Vegas owes its success to one simple fact: People do really stupid things when they're drunk . . . like, say, marry total strangers.

Las Vegas has no waiting period prior to marriage, so people will get hitched for any reason (if their blood alcohol content is above .10): because they've fallen instantly in love, because they're horny and desperate, because it's Tuesday. So, it's no surprise that Las Vegas is the wedding chapel capital of the world, offering all sorts of themed weddings replete with reams of fantasy.

If you want to get married by an Elvis impersonator—and who doesn't?!?—then chapels such as Graceland and Viva Las Vegas offer that service.

> **LIKE YOU SAID—WE TEND TO DO DUMB SHIT WHEN WE'RE FUCKED UP.**
>
> —Mike Tyson in *The Hangover*

Eager to begin eternity with that special someone but too damn lazy to get out of your car? Then head to the Little White Chapel's Tunnel of Love.

Eager to get your hands on some booty? Treasure Island offers weddings on board their pirate ship.

But Trekkies, you're shit outta luck. The Star Trek–themed chapel (no kidding) closed down, though rumors abound that it could reopen at any time. Trekkies finding sexual partners? Now *that's* fantasy.

69. HAPPILY EVER AFTER IN VEGAS (REALLY!)

While Las Vegas is famous for short-lived celebrity marriages, there have been some Hollywood hookups that have lasted longer than the average man with the average hooker.

Kirk Douglas married his second wife, Anne Buydens, on May 29, 1954, at the Sahara. Unless the craggy-voiced, dimple-chinned actor has died, then he and the second Mrs. Douglas remain married.

The third time was a charm for *Saturday Night Live* (oh, and *Golden Girls*) sensation Betty White. She married *Password* host Allen Ludden in 1963, at the Sands Hotel-Casino and the two stayed married until Ludden died of cancer in 1981. Rumors that Ashton Kutcher is planning to leave Demi Moore for Betty appear to be unfounded.

And Paul Newman and Joanne Woodward remained the perfect couple from the time they married in 1958 at the El Rancho until Newman died fifty years later.

Of course, the folks on this list are simply the exceptions that prove the rule: most Las Vegas weddings don't even last as long as those condoms you find in gas station restrooms.

70. CELEBRITY MARRIAGES THAT DIDN'T LAST

Let's start with the obvious. On January 3, 2004, at Las Vegas's Little White Wedding Chapel, Britney Spears married a childhood friend named Jason Alexander (no, not the short, bald guy from *Seinfeld*). Perhaps she was trying to reconnect to better times . . . like when she was five years old. But the nostalgic union lasted only fifty-five hours.

But Britney isn't the only celebrity to have a marriage that didn't even last as long as some hangovers. Here are some of the many, many, many celebrities whose Sin City marriages went bust:

♣ Pamela Anderson married another sex tape star, Rick Salomon, on October 6, 2007 and annulled the marriage just two months later.

♣ Gorgeous Angelina Jolie married not-so-gorgeous Billy Bob Thornton on May 5, 2000, at the Little Church of the West. The marriage lasted three years, paving the way for Brangelina and their large brood of adopted children. Whatever happened to her "Billy Bob" tattoo?

♣ Definitely-not-gay-just-ask-him actor Richard Gere married supermodel Cindy Crawford on December 12, 1991. The two divorced four years later, and Gere reportedly bought a declawed rodent soon after.

> "WE ARE HETEROSEXUAL AND MONOGAMOUS AND TAKE OUR COMMITMENT TO EACH OTHER VERY SERIOUSLY."
>
> —Cindy Crawford and Richard Gere

71. SWIMMING WITH THE SLUTS

Sure, naked women are a dime a dozen in Las Vegas, but usually they're dancing on stage or climbing poles or lining up for "viewing." But naked wet women doing the breaststroke while you splash around in the world's biggest topless pool is the sort of Sin City fun other places just dream about. The Rio came up with this tantalizing twist on the casino pool experience when it joined forces with the infamous "world's largest gentlemen's club" (see #47) to open an "adult-themed" swimming pool complete with three waterfalls, and lots of nearly nude Sapphire girls.

At $30 for a male guest and more than $500 for a cabana, it was fun for all while it lasted. Unfortunately, the pool has since been closed "indefinitely," due to numerous arrests for prostitution and drugs. Imagine that.

So if swimming with beautiful bare-chested babes from the Sapphire Gentleman's Club is your idea of a fun afternoon in the desert sun, well, sorry to say you have missed your chance. You'll have to settle for one of the other, less notorious adult-themed pools in town.

TOP ADULTS-ONLY POOLS IN VEGAS

Don your thong—or your skimpiest bikini—and check these out:

- ♠ Bare at The Mirage
- ♠ Venus at Caesars
- ♠ Moorea at Mandalay Bay
- ♠ Wet Republic at the MGM Grand
- ♠ Rehab at the Hard Rock
- ♠ TAO Beach at The Venetian

72. THE CHAPEL OF THE FLOWERS: THE TRADITIONALIST'S CHOICE

One of the oldest wedding chapels on the Strip is the Chapel of the Flowers. Formerly known as the Little Chapel of the Flowers, it's been remodeled many times over the years, which is why it isn't so little anymore. The charming white-steepled building is one of the most traditional chapels—and the one most often rated the best wedding chapel in Las Vegas.

Traditional, of course, is a relative term—relative to nothing in the rest of the world. Chapel of the Flowers is known for being the place where:

- ♣ Some 5,000 couples of the 110,000 people who marry in Las Vegas every year say "I do."
- ♣ Reality TV show *Happily Ever Faster* is shot. It's a riot of a show revealing the behind the scenes chaos that is the wedding business in Vegas, as run by owners Jason and Holly Myers, who claim to be happily married themselves. Watch the show and see for yourself.
- ♣ The Killers' drummer Ronnie Vanucci worked as a photographer. Ronnie shot weddings there while recording the group's debut album *Hot Fuss*.

Part Three

GLUTTONY

CHAPTER 8

FOOD

73. A BIT OF THE OLD IN-N-OUT

In-N-Out may sound like the name of one of Nevada's many legal brothels, but actually it's a chain of marginally Christian and devilishly tasty
burger joints with employees that have an eerie resemblance to Stepford
children (i.e., they seem like perfectly behaved and groomed robots).

In-N-Out Burger, launched in 1948 in Irvine, California, expanded
eastward to Las Vegas in 1992. Its hallmarks are fresh food, android teen
employees, and clandestine Bible verses. See, look carefully under that
milkshake cup. Do you see what's printed there? *Proverbs 3:5.* That verse
talks about how you should trust in the Lord and not listen to your own
stupid, sinful thoughts . . . not even in Sin City.

> ONE OF THE TRUE GREAT THINGS ABOUT LOS ANGELES [AND, IT
> SEEMS REASONABLE TO ASSUME, LAS VEGAS] IS IN-N-OUT BURGER.
> —Tom Hanks

In-N-Out Burger seems like a throwback to a simpler time, but it
has earned a few cool points by being mentioned prominently in the
non-Harold-and-Kumar stoner classic, *The Big Lebowski.* So, even though
you've come to Vegas for gambling, hookups, and beer, you should take
time to visit one of the Western United States's best places to pig out.

74. FATBURGER

We've got a simple solution for all you white and nerdy folks looking for some instant street cred, so you can "represent" your suburban hood, yo. Just pick up a Fatburger cap when you visit Sin City.

Lovie Yancey launched Mr. Fatburger in Los Angeles in 1947. She chose a name that suggested a hamburger designed to strike fear in the hearts of anorexics everywhere. By 1952, "Mr." was gone, and Fatburger was on its way to becoming a successful franchise.

> " TRY FATBURGER FROM NOW ON. "
>
> —*The Fast and the Furious*

For whatever reason—perhaps because the chain was founded by an African American—rappers, gangstas, and just plain G's have adopted Fatburger and made it a swagg icon. The late Notorious B.I.G., for example, once opined, "If I wanna squirt her, [I] take her to Fatburger." Ice Cube—when he was still straight up street—once made the restaurant an essential ingredient of a good day: "Two in the morning, got the Fatburger." In addition, rapper Kanye West and rapper/actress Queen Latifah own Fatburger franchises.

75. EARTH TO WHITE CASTLE: GET YOUR ASS TO SIN CITY

Hey, White Castle, get your head out of your behind. Sure, your slyders and belly bombs are celebrated the world over for offering succor to the totally wasted. When one is too high to fly and the munchies are at one's door like the proverbial big bad wolf, you are the perfect antidote to stoner cravings. Just ask Harold and Kumar! When one is drunk but clinging to that last vestige of sanity—gotta stave off that hangover—you can coat an alcohol-filled stomach better than Teflon coats a frying pan.

But you are totally missing out.

People may go out of their way for a sackful of slyders, but they aren't going all the way to Wisconsin if they're getting totally wasted in Sin City. What do you have against the West Coast? Why are you denying drunk and stoned people in Las Vegas their inalienable right to a belly bomber? Hell, why are you denying yourselves the sacks full of profits to be made from the munchies-stricken denizens of Sin City?

Come to Vegas and all will be forgiven!

> **IT'S A FUCKING SAUSAGEFEST IN HERE, BROS. LET'S GET SOME POONTANG. *THEN* WE'LL GO TO WHITE CASTLE.**
>
> —Neil Patrick Harris in *Harold & Kumar Go to White Castle*

76. MEDITERRANEAN CAFÉ AND HOOKAH LOUNGE

Sure, the Mediterranean Café has your typical range of Middle Eastern dishes—your falafel, your stuffed grape leaves, your baba ganoush—but the real attraction is its hookah lounge.

If you've seen *Alice in Wonderland*—the Disney cartoon movie—then you've seen a hookah. It's basically a giant bong with all sorts of fancy tubes wrapped around it. Most head shops sell them as glass-blown "tobacco water" pipes.

At the Hookah Lounge (Note: Mediterranean Café has trademarked that name), you and your buddies can smoke a hookah and feel like rebels or something. A "Hookah Man" comes to your table and offers you your choice of flavored tobacco. Once the proper flavor is chosen, the tobacco is, basically, placed in water, and you smoke it through one of the hookah's pipes.

What's the attraction? According to the Mediterranean Café, hookah smoking is an experience with a long, colorful history. In truth, it's just cool to look like you're smoking a giant bong in public instead of in your parents' basement.

> " THE LOOK OF AMAZEMENT USUALLY FOLLOWS AFTER THE FIRST PUFF. "
> —*Hookahlounge.com*

77. ALL YOU CAN EAT 'TIL YOU PUKE BUFFET

Back in the 1940s, Beldon Katleman was looking for a way to keep people up all night long at the original Hotel El Rancho Vegas—the first casino resort on the Strip. So he came up with the Midnight Chuck Wagon Buffet, a spread that although modest by today's standards was still appealing enough to keep the customers coming, especially at their bargain price: All You Can Eat for $1.

Sixty years later, buffets are as much a part of the Las Vegas experience as slot machines. Almost every gambling resort has one—from the more affordable Ports O' Call Buffet at the Gold Coast to the delightful gastronomic tour of France served up at Le Village Buffet at the Paris Las Vegas, which features authentic buffets from each of the country's five provinces.

But the best buffet in Vegas is generally acknowledged to be the Carnival World Buffet at the Rio, which boasts more than three hundred dishes, from sushi and pizza to seafood and barbeque. Not to mention the seventy kinds of pastries and nine kinds of gelato made from scratch every day.

78. LINE UP FOR GLUTTONY

Four out of every five tourists gorge themselves at a buffet in Las Vegas—a total of more than 29 million buffet diners a year. Excuse us while we belch.

> ## WHO'S FEEDING THE TOURISTS?
>
> In Las Vegas, 15 percent of the workforce work in food preparation and service—nearly double the national average of 8.6 percent. That's more than 120,000 people, including 30,000 waiters, 12,000 cooks, 9,000 dishwashers and 9,000 bartenders, according to the Bureau of Labor Statistics.

79. THE ULTIMATE BEANO BURRITO

How big is a *big* burrito? Well, at the Sahara's NASCAR Café, it's a two-foot long, six-pound monster that goes for a whopping $20—unless you can eat the so-called B3 Burrito all by yourself. If you can, then it's yours for free—as long as you do any subsequent farting elsewhere.

The bonus: Perform this crazy feat of consumption and you get a lifetime of free roller coaster rides at the Sahara. Not that you'll be in any shape to ride one after eating that massive burrito.

The caveat: Only a handful of determined diners have succeeded in downing the entire *two gallons'* worth of tortillas, beans, shredded beef, cheese, olives, guacamole, sour cream, and enchilada sauce.

80. DON'T TELL THE SHRIMP HUGGERS

Shrimp is America's favorite seafood, having bumped tuna to second place more than a decade ago. Americans down more than four pounds of the sweet marine meat per capita every year—until they come to Vegas, at which time their shrimp habit morphs into an addiction.

Shrimp is one of the most popular staples of the ubiquitous Las Vegas buffet, where tourists line up to eat their weight in crustaceans—some 60,000 pounds a day, more than all the rest of the country combined.

Ninety percent of this shrimp comes from overseas, most notably China, Thailand, India, and Indonesia, whose shrimp farms have come under the gun by environmentalists for displacing mangrove forests. Most of our domestic shrimp comes from the Gulf of Mexico, now under threat from the BP oil spill. But no matter where it comes from or how it's caught, the shrimp served in the desert city must be flown or trucked in, racking up millions of barrels of oil in the process.

Watchdog organizations advise people not to eat farm-raised shrimp, and to discourage restaurants from serving it. Las Vegas—one of the least green places on earth, literally and figuratively—is not listening.

81. THE ORIGINAL SHRIMP COCKTAIL

The Golden Gate Hotel & Casino may be the oldest and smallest hotel in the Fremont Street Experience—better known as downtown Las Vegas—but it remains king of the shrimp cocktail. The 1906 landmark has changed hands and names and been renovated and expanded over the years, but its dedication to shrimp has never wavered. The Golden Gate introduced the first 50-cent Original Shrimp Cocktail in 1959. It'll cost you $1.99 now, but you'll still get a generous helping of the whitest, meatiest shrimp from the cold waters of Washington, Oregon, Alaska, and the East Coast, served up prettily in their trademark tulip glass.

82. DROWNING IN CHOCOLATE

After stuffing yourself to the gills on all that shrimp, you'd think you'd have no room for dessert. Think again. If Las Vegas promises anything, it's excess. And excess is what brings chocoholics the world over to the Bellagio, where the world's biggest chocolate fountain spills two tons of chocolate twenty-four hours a day. Designed by renowned Montreal glass artist Michel Mailhot, this 27-foot high marvel features 2,100 pounds of streaming confectionary grade white, medium, and dark chocolate, cascading in elegant streams from one of twenty-five hand-crafted glass vessels to another. Two years in the making, this awesome display of chocolate extravagance graces the entryway of the Jean-Philippe Patisserie, World Pastry Champion Chef Jean-Philippe Maury's European-style bakery extraordinaire. Dessert lovers flock to this sugary oasis, known for its signature chocolates, cookies, cakes, candies, and crepes. But even among such delicious delights, this magnificent chocolate confectionary centerpiece stands out.

THE SWEETEST VICE OF THEM ALL

Willy Wonka aside, as vices in Las Vegas go, chocolate is fairly innocuous. The biggest risks to chocoholism may be obesity, tooth decay, and depression. But chocoholics often prefer to cite the benefits of dark chocolate, which studies indicate may reduce the risk of heart attack and stroke, according to the *Journal of Nutrition*.

Willy Wonka himself sang the praises of the chocolate waterfall—and you can't help but believe he was right when you see this one.

> "NO OTHER FACTORY IN THE WORLD MIXES ITS CHOCOLATE BY WATERFALL. . . . BUT IT'S THE ONLY WAY IF YOU WANT IT JUST RIGHT."
> —Gene Wilder as Willy Wonka in *Willy Wonka & the Chocolate Factory*

83. THE $5,000 LUNCH

If you want to treat a friend to lunch and you're jonesing for a good burger, then head on over to the Fleur de Lys Restaurant at Mandalay Bay. In this *fantastique* French restaurant, you'll find Gallic classics like filet mignon and onion soup along with the most expensive burgers in town.

Let's say you just won Mega Bucks and can actually afford the most expensive burgers in town. Then order the FleurBurger 5000, *s'il vous plaît*.

That's 5000 as in $5,000. *Alors,* for $5,000 these are very special burgers: two Kobe beef patties on brioche truffle buns smothered in foie gras, black truffles, and truffle sauce. (Yes, two—that's why you bring a friend.) And to wash all that *tres* pricey ground beef down—a bottle of 1990 Chateau Petrus wine comes with lunch. *À votre santé!*

> " A HAMBURGER BY ANY OTHER NAME COSTS TWICE AS MUCH. "
>
> —Evan Esar

84. THE $6,000 LUNCH

If you think dropping five grand for lunch is slumming, then forget Mandalay Bay, and head over to the Palms. Here your burger lunch will cost you six grand—if you're dining solo. You'll have to add six bucks if you bring a friend.

Okay, we know what you're thinking: That simply does not add up. *Au contraire,* my friend. At the Palms, they're not serving up Kobe beef; they're going for gold with Carl's Jr. Yeah, you heard that right. The $6,000 Combo Meal features a $6 Carl's Jr. burger—and a twenty-four-year-old bottle of French Bordeaux. Throw in another burger and you're talking another six bucks. Of course, you'll have to share the wine.

> " SOMEBODY LEFT THE CORK OUT OF MY LUNCH. "
>
> —W.C. Fields

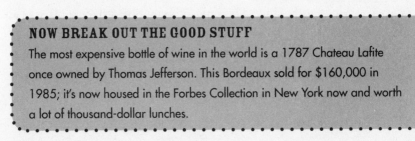

NOW BREAK OUT THE GOOD STUFF

The most expensive bottle of wine in the world is a 1787 Chateau Lafite once owned by Thomas Jefferson. This Bordeaux sold for $160,000 in 1985; it's now housed in the Forbes Collection in New York now and worth a lot of thousand-dollar lunches.

CHAPTER 9

DRUGS

85. CALAMITY JAYNE, LAS VEGAS STYLE

She's a cowpunk outlaw. She's the woman who brought Iggy to Las Vegas. She's the woman who used her popular rock club to launder drug money. Unlike the real Calamity Jane, the famous frontierswoman and scout, the first two statements about Las Vegas's Calamity Jayne (born Claudia Rae) are true, but the third? Well, it depends on whom you ask. True, Jayne *did* accept a plea bargain related to money laundering, but she claims—and perhaps, honestly—that she didn't really know what was going on at her immortal music venue, Calamity Jayne's Nashville Nevada.

> I'M NO SAINT. I'VE TRIED IT ALL. BUT EVEN THOUGH I LOOK WILD, I'VE BEEN CLEAR ALL MY LIFE.
>
> —Calamity Jayne

When the Nashville Nevada opened in the 1980s, Las Vegas was a musical joke. "Real" bands stayed away from a city known for has-beens and lounge lizards. But Jayne managed to bring in everyone from Depeche Mode to Sublime. The one and only time Nirvana played Las Vegas occurred at the Nashville Nevada.

Then the wheels fell off the bus. Jayne became linked with Carl Whittenburg, an eccentric contractor who moonlighted as a marijuana and cocaine smuggler for various drug cartels. Ultimately, the feds swooped in, closed down the club, arrested Whittenburg and Jayne, and she spent eighteen months in prison.

86. ECSTASY AND THE ISRAELI MOB

Oy vey. You mean there's an *Israeli* mob, too? After Las Vegas finally (mostly) got rid of the "real" Italian mafia members (many of which, to be fair, were Jewish), there's reportedly a new gang of homicidal misfits in town.

The "original" Sin City mobsters had and fulfilled big visions. They built hotels. They skimmed millions from casinos. They whacked one another when they felt like it. The "new" Israeli mafia, by contrast, sup-posedly works more like a specialty house.

Las Vegas has an amazing nightlife scene, of course. And what do you need to enjoy the nightlife? Boobies. But that's not all! You also need drugs—especially ecstasy. What's the fun in just enjoying music, dancing, and meaningless hookups, unless you also can tweak until the dawn's early light?

So, many claim that's the Israeli mob's job: providing drugs to Las Vegas partiers. They've been on the local, state, and federal radar at least since the dawn of the millennium.

And apparently the Israeli mob isn't just interested in drugs. Some say it also extorts money from Las Vegas–area businesses.

87. THE DEATH OF JOHN ENTWISTLE

Who knew? He seemed so boring. Yet, the man considered the greatest rock bassist of all time died, well, a rock star's death in Las Vegas. Appropri-ately, The Who's John Entwistle died at the Hard Rock Hotel and Casino.

On June 27, 2002, when news began filtering out that Entwistle had been found dead in his hotel room, reports indicated the cause of death was a heart attack. Well, sure. He was relatively *old* for a rocker (fifty-eight), and heart attacks have been known to happen to aging people, especially hard-partying rockers.

> JOHN ENTWISTLE [WAS] THE QUIETEST MAN IN PRIVATE BUT THE LOUDEST MAN ON STAGE.
>
> —Bill Wyman

For the most important portion of his career, Entwistle played beside Keith Moon, the wildest of rock's wild men, who died of an overdose in 1978. Compared to Moon, the always silent Entwistle seemed like a choir boy. But, as Gomer Pyle used to say, "Surprise! Surprise!"

Entwistle *did* die of a heart attack, but the heart attack was brought on by cocaine. *And* Entwistle was discovered dead by the "stripper/groupie" he had taken to bed the night before The Who's first show as part of their new American tour. All right, John! You weren't such a square after all! But you didn't die before you got *old*.

88. THIS IS LAS VEGAS ON DRUGS

Just because you live in Vegas doesn't mean you're addicted to gambling, booze, sex, and drugs. But the odds that you are addicted to one of those things are better here than anywhere else in the country.

It really shouldn't surprise anyone that a place that celebrates gambling, booze, sex, and drugs might prove a difficult environment for those prone to addiction. In fact, substance abuse is more pervasive in the state of Nevada than anywhere else in America. According to the Bureau of Alcohol and Drug Abuse, 13 percent of the Nevada population need help fighting an addiction. And it's estimated that helping addicts fight their battles costs the state more than a billion dollars a year in heath care, legal, education, and lost productivity costs.

> **WE'RE #1 DRUGGIES**
> Nevada ranks number one in drug dependency, according to the National Survey of Household Drug Use.

" THERE I WAS. ALONE IN LAS VEGAS, COMPLETELY TWISTED ON DRUGS, NO CASH, NO STORY FOR THE MAGAZINE, AND ON TOP OF EVERYTHING ELSE, A GIGANTIC GOD DAMNED HOTEL BILL TO DEAL WITH. "

—Johnny Depp as Raoul Duke in *Fear and Loathing in Las Vegas*

89. METH MADNESS

If you think of crystal meth as a white trash drug you predominantly find in run-down trailer parks in Tennessee or Arkansas or California, well, you're right. But to complete that pretty picture, you have to come to—where else?—Las Vegas. In Sin City, meth use is rampant. In fact, the entire state of Nevada is suffering through what is arguably the most serious methamphetamine crisis in the nation.

The ramifications are widespread. Meth use fuels much of the crime here—from petty theft and drug charges to child abuse and homicide. It's destroying not only the lives of the individual drug users, but also the lives of their children and other family members, as well as entire communities.

The crisis prompted the filming and showing of *Crystal Darkness: Meth's Deadly Assault on Nevada's Youth*, a brutally honest and disturbing documentary aimed at discouraging meth use among teens.

> **TWEAKED TEENS**
>
> One in five high school juniors in the state of Nevada reported using meth-amphetamine, according to the Nevada Department of Health and Human Services.

90. CALLING ALL TWEAKERS

There are more people on meth per capita in the state of Nevada than anywhere in the country. According to the Substance Abuse and Mental Health Services Administration:

♣ More people here have taken methamphetamine in the past thirty days.

♣ More people here have taken methamphetamine in the past year.

♣ More people here have taken methamphetamine in their lifetime.

Given these outrageous facts, you just have to wonder: Who here isn't getting high?

> **THE DOPE IN DOPAMINE**
>
> What makes meth such a powerful addictive drug is its effect on dopamine levels in the brain. Dopamine makes us feel good—and the higher the level of dopamine in the brain, the better we feel. It's why we feel good when we exercise. The typical runner's high is all about the release of 100 to 200 units of dopamine. But get tweaked, and crystal meth will flood your brain with some 1,200 units of dopamine—giving you the most euphoric high pharmacologically available, even better than cocaine. Ultimately, however, crystal methamphetamine has real potential to screw up your brain, impairing judgment and motor coordination, as well as inducing psychosis and violence.

91. LAS VEGAS'S MOST FAMOUS METH HEAD

One of Las Vegas's favorite native sons, "Wild Child" Andre Agassi was at one time apparently wild about crystal meth. The tennis star turned philanthropist was born in Las Vegas in 1970 and has been a staunch supporter of his hometown all his life. Along the way he has raised some $60 million for disadvantaged youth in Southern Nevada.

But he shocked his fellow Las Vegans—and the rest of the world—in 2009 when he admitted in his *New York Times* bestselling autobiography *Open* that he'd had a crystal meth problem in the late 1990s, saying that it was a period in his life when he needed help.

Now retired, Agassi is married to tennis great Steffi Graf; they live in Las Vegas with their two children. He continues to devote much of his time to the Andre Agassi Charitable Foundation, which supports Boys and Girls Clubs in the region, has established a tuition-free charter school for disadvantaged kids, a home for abused children, and a facility for special-needs youth, among other things.

> I CAN'T SPEAK TO ADDICTION, BUT A LOT OF PEOPLE WOULD SAY THAT IF YOU'RE USING ANYTHING AS AN ESCAPE, YOU HAVE A PROBLEM.
>
> —Andre Agassi, on his meth use in the late 1990s

CHAPTER 10

ALCOHOL

92. BUBBLY TO THE MAX

Everyone loves champagne—and Las Vegans are no different. Of course, Vegas being Vegas, champagne sparkles even more brightly here. Consider:

BEEF AND BUBBLY

When the fabled Caesar's Palace first opened its doors in 1966, visitors to the one-of-a-kind casino washed down two tons of filet mignon with some 50,000 flutes of champagne.

> TOO MUCH OF ANYTHING IS BAD, BUT TOO MUCH CHAMPAGNE IS JUST RIGHT.
>
> —Mark Twain

CHEERS, JAY-Z!

There's a 15-liter bottle of Ace of Spades champagne with the popular singer's name on it at TAO—and it can be yours for only $100,000. According to the manager at TAO, there are only two such bottles on the planet—and only this bubbly boasts Jay-Z's autograph. If you've been living in a cave, then you won't know that the champagne takes center stage in Jay-Z's 2006 hit song and video, "Show Me What You Got."

93. THE MAYOR'S DRINK

When it comes to mayors there are few as colorful as Oscar B. Goodman. The three-time chief executive is a former criminal defense attorney whose notorious clients included such reputed mobsters as Meyer Lansky, Frank "Lefty" Rosenthal, and Anthony "Tony the Ant" Spilotro (see #147). Billing himself as the world's happiest mayor, Goodman has reveled in his role since he first won the job in 1999.

Goodman also loves gin. In 2002 he accepted the role of spokesperson for Bombay Sapphire Gin—and donated his $100,000 paycheck to charity. The public may have approved of that, but the climate changed in 2005, when Goodman told a classroom full of fourth graders at Jo Mackey Elementary School that if he were stranded on a desert island he'd want "a showgirl and a bottle of Bombay Sapphire Gin" with him. He followed that up by naming the selfsame gin as one of his "hobbies." Parents and school officials were not amused.

> I'M THE GEORGE WASHINGTON OF MAYORS. I CAN'T TELL A LIE. IF THEY DIDN'T WANT THE ANSWER, THE KID SHOULDN'T HAVE ASKED THE QUESTION.
>
> —Oscar Goodman

OSCAR GOES TO THE MOVIES

Oscar B. Goodman isn't just a mayor; he's a movie star. In 1995, he played a cameo role as himself in the film *Casino*, the mob story set in Las Vegas starring Robert DeNiro, Joe Pesci, and Sharon Stone and directed by our favorite mobster movie maven Martin Scorsese. Goodman later appeared in *Looney Toons: Back in Action* as well.

94. THE JOYS OF SUNDAY MORNING BOOZE SHOPPING

Gleaming amber and blue bottles. Gin and vodka on the supermarket shelves, shining like diamonds. It's Sunday morning in Las Vegas. Who needs Jesus?

Unlike practically every other municipality in the United States, Las Vegas couldn't give two shits that you're here to drink, drink, drink. In fact, the city encourages overindulgence. It's a simple equation, really: Drunk = no common sense = gamble away life savings.

In Las Vegas, booze is just another aisle in the grocery store, and it's available 24/7. Perhaps this is why Sin City is so popular with Southerners. Southern States treat alcohol like it's still in the grip of Prohibition. Craving Southern Comfort on a Sunday? Sorry, y'all. The liquor store is closed. So, when in Vegas, give a rebel yell as you reach for that bottle of Rebel Yell whiskey while everyone else slinks off to church. You're on vacation, son!

95. DON'T BE A SUCKER

We repeat: Bottled alcohol is available at any grocery store in Las Vegas. Most chains even have their own generic brands of popular alcohol. If you buy liquor on the Strip, you will be ripped off. Fair warning. Settle for being a sucker in the casino.

96. BARFLY PARADISES

Fans of the late Charles Bukowski have plenty to celebrate in Las Vegas. Bukowski—a self-professed barfly—wrote novels, stories, and poems about being an inveterate drunk who spent most of his time in run-down bars. While most folks would call someone like this a loser, many people came to venerate Bukowski as some sort of enlightened soul. Go figure.

Although Bukowski was associated with Los Angeles, he would have felt right at home in barfly paradises all over Sin City. Unlike most cities,

Las Vegas has no last call. Bars are open 24/7. Therefore, you can't hawk up a loogie without hitting a gin palace. Aw, who the hell are we kidding? These places aren't palaces. They're shitholes, but they are shitholes with a certain *je ne sais quois*.

> ❝ WE HAVE WASTED HISTORY LIKE A BUNCH OF DRUNKS SHOOTING DICE BACK OF THE MEN'S CRAPPER OF THE LOCAL BAR. ❞
> —Charles Bukowski

You'll find any number of places that offer low-fi atmosphere, really cheap booze, and some of the most interesting burned-out folks you would ever care to meet. All you've got to do is head out on Charleston Boulevard toward Red Rock Canyon; go to practically any spot near the defunct Huntridge Theater; or go down Boulder Highway just a few blocks from Glitter Gulch.

Did we mention the really cheap booze?

97. VINCE NEIL BLOWS (ABOVE THE LEGAL LIMIT)

Some guys never learn. You would think that one tragic and fatal accident would make you think twice about drinking and driving, right? Well, Motley Crue frontman, Vince Neil, seemingly didn't get that memo.

In an apparent (bizarre and insensitive) nod to Neil's first drunk-driving experience—a 1984 crash that killed Hanoi Rocks drummer Nicholas Dingley and left both occupants of the other car in a vegetative state—Motley Crue released a box set entitled, *Music to Crash Your Car To*.

On June 28, 2010, Neil (allegedly) was driving along Desert Inn Road when he was pulled over by Las Vegas police on suspicion of drunk driving. As of this writing, sentencing is pending.

98. PEPPERMILL'S FIRESIDE LOUNGE

Ahh! We've wandered into the 1970s! Can we blame this on a hot tub time machine? Nope. We've just wandered into Peppermill's Fireside Lounge.

While some adjustments have been made to this old-style lounge over the years (giant flat-screen televisions, for example), the Peppermill is still one of the greatest places in Las Vegas to make out . . . and that's saying a lot. This is Sin City, after all!

> MANY COUPLES COME TO THE FIRESIDE JUST TO MAKE OUT. THEY PAW AT EACH OTHER LIKE CRAZED LEMURS.
>
> —Geoff Carter, *Vegas.com*

Why? One word: Darkness! You and your sweetheart—or temporary hookup—can sink into the cozy booths near the signature fire pit, get totally bombed on girlie drinks, and make out like you've never made out before.

The Peppermill is a branch of Reno's Peppermill, perhaps *that* city's swankiest casino resort. In Vegas, the place seems more like a throwback to a simpler time . . . a time when your biggest STD concern was merely gonorrhea.

99. THE MUCHO BUCKS MARTINI

The martini may have been born of bathtub gin, but it's come a long way since the Roaring Twenties. At the Body English club in the Hard Rock Hotel and Casino, the classic cocktail gets a magnificent—and mighty expensive—makeover.

The Aristocrat Martini boasts three priceless ingredients: Remy Martin Louis XIII Cognac, 150-year-old Gran Marnier, and a splash of Dom Perignon. You can sip this elegant concoction for only $2,000.

Or you can make it at home on the cheap: just pour two ounces of your favorite cognac and half an ounce of Gran Marnier into a martini glass, then add a splash of sparkling wine.

"HE KNOWS JUST HOW I LIKE MY MARTINI—FULL OF ALCOHOL."

—Homer Simpson

At Body English, the Aristocrat comes with a ruby-and-diamond encrusted swizzle stick that you can take home with you as a souvenir. But you can use a jelly jar and a toothpick at home, if that's what you want, you aristocrat you.

100. BEER HEAVEN

There's nothing like a cold one on a hot day—which may explain why the State of Nevada leads the nation in beer consumption per capita. That's four gallons of beer per person per year in the Silver State—and God knows how much per tourist.

> **THE BREWSKI BOYS**
>
> Eighty percent of the beer chugged in America is chugged by men. Men also do most of the belching, farting, and crotch-grabbing in America, too. Go figure.

No surprise, really. After all, availability is not a problem (see #96).

If you're into quality, rather than quantity, then who are you and what are you doing in Vegas?

Still, if you *are* serious about that quality thing, check out the suds at Sin City Microbrewery, the Ellis Island Casino bar, or Big Dog's Café and Casino.

> WITHOUT QUESTION, THE GREATEST INVENTION IN THE HISTORY OF MANKIND IS BEER. OH, I GRANT YOU THAT THE WHEEL WAS ALSO A FINE INVENTION, BUT THE WHEEL DOES NOT GO NEARLY AS WELL WITH PIZZA.

—Dave Barry

101. HOW DRUNK IS TOO DRUNK TO GET HITCHED?

Urban legends aside, the Clark County Marriage License Bureau insists that no marriage licenses are granted to drunks, no matter how famous they are.

That's their story and they are sticking to it. Even when outrageous celebs such as basketball bad boy Dennis Rodman and *Baywatch* babe Carmen Electra get married under questionable sobriety at the Little Chapel of the Flowers in Las Vegas in 1998.

> WE DON'T ISSUE A LICENSE IF THEY'RE INTOXICATED, NO MATTER WHO THEY ARE.

—Cheryl Vernon, supervisor of the Clark County (Nevada) Marriage License Bureau

Rodman filed for an annulment only nine days later, claiming that he had been too drunk to know what he was doing. Shortly thereafter he recanted, and insisted that it was love not liquor that led him to the chapel, saying "I apologize for any false statements given on my behalf regarding my marriage to Carmen Electra."

In any case, the marriage ended in divorce in 1999.

102. HAVE A DRINK ON VEGAS

Nothing fuels gambling like alcohol. That's why the drinks are free in casinos. It may seem obvious, but every day tourists come to Vegas intending to see the sights—and not lose any money.

But before you know it, you're hanging out at the dollar slots and a cute cocktail waitress with legs as long as Virginia Hill comes along and wham! A couple of free mojitos later, you're laughing with your new best friend from Omaha as you rack up your own equivalent of the national debt.

Why? Because booze makes you stupid. Seriously. When you imbibe too much, the alcohol blocks vital messages on the way to your brain— you know, the ones telling you not to bet everything you've got (in Vegas *and* back at home) on video poker.

So go ahead and have a free drink—just remember there's nothing free about Las Vegas.

> A WEEKEND IN VEGAS WITHOUT GAMBLING AND DRINKING IS JUST LIKE BEING A BORN-AGAIN CHRISTIAN.

—Artie Lange

Part Four
SLOTH

CHAPTER 11

CONS

103. DOES ANYBODY REALLY KNOW WHAT TIME IT IS?

There are no clocks in the casinos—and there's a reason why. The gambling gods want you to gamble—and casinos are designed to encourage you to gamble all you've got—and more. These tricks of the gambling trade are based on psychologically sound principles, i.e., they work. They work so well that Las Vegas rakes in billions of dollars a year, in good times and bad.

Banning timepieces are part of their carefully concocted plan. Clocks are a ticking reminder of the real world where you are a responsible person with bills to pay and money in the bank. A casino is another world, one that exists outside time and space, where you are an adventurous person with bridges to burn and money in your pocket.

No clocks, no worries, nowhere to be but here. Gambling.

104. LOST IN CASINOLAND

If you get lost every time you set foot in a casino, don't blame your sense of direction. Casinos are labyrinthine structures designed to keep people inside playing games and losing money as long as humanly possible. That's why you can never find your way out. All of the usual methods by which we find our way in strange or new places—signs, landmarks, entrances, and exits—are conspicuously absent. All roads lead right back to the slot machines and blackjack tables where you began—and odds are where you will remain, long enough to lose your shirt.

105. LOTS OF SLOTS

There are some 200,000 slot machines in Las Vegas alone. Bring plenty of coins.

106. WHERE'S THE LADIES' ROOM?

Another carefully plotted facet of casino design is the placing of such essential customer services as bathrooms, restaurants, and cashiers. They're always located deep within the casino; getting there requires passing through the gaming areas. The more you roam inside the casino, the more likely you are to stop and gamble. It's a safe bet—and one the house always wins.

> YOUR BEST CHANCE TO GET A ROYAL FLUSH IN A CASINO IS IN THE BATHROOM.
>
> —V.P. Pappy

107. BRIGHT LIGHTS, BIG GAMBLE

Casinos are a fascinating blend of stimulating distraction and make-yourself-at home appeal. The distraction keeps you from thinking about the ramifications of your actions however rash. And the welcoming ambiance helps you feel like you belong—and pampered.

> THEY [SLOT MACHINES] SIT THERE LIKE YOUNG COURTESANS, PROMISING PLEASURES UNDREAMED OF, YOUR DEEPEST DESIRES FULFILLED, ALL LUSTS SATIATED.
>
> —Frank Scoblete

In the gaming areas, the carpet is thick and heavily patterned, the music soothing, the ceilings low, the lighting soft, and the upkeep perfection. Your home away from home—only with an army of staffers dedicated to keeping you happy.

108. MORNING ALL NIGHT LONG

There are no windows in casinos, just as there are no clocks. This helps maintain the illusion of timelessness. Day becomes night and night becomes day—one long round-the-clock party of drinking and gambling and whooping it up.

> ### 88.8 HOURS AND COUNTING...
> The typical tourist spends 3.7 nights during the average stay in Las Vegas.

For many people, it's this fun-filled marathon vision of Las Vegas that draws them to Sin City—and keeps them coming back. If they ever get home.

> " IT'S A CORNY OLD GAG ABOUT LAS VEGAS, THE TEMPORAL CITY IF THERE EVER WAS ONE, TRYING TO CAMOUFLAGE THE HOURS AND RETARD THE DAWN, WHEN EVERYBODY KNOWS THAT IF YOU'RE FEELING LUCKY YOU'RE REALLY FEELING TIME IN ITS RAWEST FORM, AND IF YOU'RE NOT FEELING LUCKY, THEY'VE GOT A CLOCK AT THE BUS STATION. "
>
> —Michael Herr

109. HIGH ROLLER HEAVEN

The more money you lose in Las Vegas, the better they treat you. Drop a bundle in the casino and they'll comp you free rooms, free meals, free shows, free limousines, free VIP passes, and more. Even the more moderate gamblers hanging out at the more modest casinos enjoy similar perks. Repeat business is critical to the continued health of the gaming industry. With increased competition from casinos in other states, as well as abroad, Las Vegas gambling operations are doing all they can to attract high rollers—and to keep them coming back.

THE HIGH ROLLERS THAT ROARED

When the MGM Grand opened in 1993, the entrance was built as a huge lion's open mouth, in keeping with the corporate symbol of the roaring lion. But superstitious Asian high rollers refused to walk through the entrance, in the fear that it would bring them bad luck. They stayed away—and the MGM Grand lost countless millions in valuable Asian business. They corrected their mistake, but it cost them millions of dollars to reconfigure the entrance, which now features a 45-foot, 100,000-pound bronze statue of a lion on a pedestal. You don't have to walk through it.

110. JUST A JACKPOT AWAY

Nothing keeps a gambler gambling longer than close calls. "I nearly hit the jackpot this time," you think, and so you keep on rolling the dice, throwing down the cards, hitting the slots, spinning the roulette wheel.

But all the Las Vegas games are designed to hook you in with small wins at the start—only to bleed you dry over the long haul. The house always wins—sooner or later. So that rush you feel early on fades—and can turn to despair when you're out of chips. So quit while you're ahead.

If you ever get ahead.

> IN VEGAS, I GOT INTO A LONG ARGUMENT WITH THE MAN AT THE ROULETTE WHEEL OVER WHAT I CONSIDERED TO BE AN ODD NUMBER.

—Stephen Wright

111. AND THE WINNER IS . . . NEVADA!

In Nevada, casino gambling revenue typically tops $12 billion a year. That's the good news. The bad news is that Las Vegas depends on tourism for its survival more than any other city in America.

In a new study by Applied Analysis, Las Vegas tops the tourism dependency scale with Orlando and Atlantic City close behind. While Orlando hosts the most tourists per year, and Atlantic City the most per capita, Las Vegas depends the most on tourism for the lion's share of annual employment and wages. (Source: Las Vegas Convention and Visitors Authority)

> FOR A LOSER, VEGAS IS THE MEANEST TOWN ON EARTH.
>
> —Hunter S. Thompson

112. LIFE DOWN IN THE DRAINS

Las Vegas has more than 300 miles of water runoff tunnels underneath it, a subway from Hell, filled with people who aren't going anywhere. Dozens, possibly hundreds, of the homeless live in the tunnels, near entrances to such hoity toity properties as the Luxor and Excalibur.

> THE INSTINCT OF THE CITY . . . IS TO IGNORE STUFF THAT CAN BE CONSTRUED AS NEGATIVE PRESS AND KIND OF HIGHLIGHT OTHER THINGS ABOUT THE CITY.
>
> —Matthew O'Brien

Journalist Matthew O'Brien first brought public attention to the so-called "bat caves" underneath glitzy Sin City: "It's not all bad for the folks in the tunnels. Some have scrounged up nice casino castoffs, such as queen-sized beds, and decorated their portions of the tunnels with them. There's just one problem. When it rains—somewhere between twenty-five and fifty days a year—the tunnels do their job, and those who don't have much lose what little they've got."

But don't worry about it. Throw away that half-eaten hot dog. Throw up most of your beer. This is America, baby! Who cares about the homeless? At least they've got somewhere to stay about 315 days a year!

113. BEYOND HUMAN GAMBLING: HEAVEN'S GATE VISITS VEGAS

In February of 1997, a group of folks arrived at the Stratosphere Hotel and Casino on the Strip, dropped some two thousand bucks on gambling and more than $250 on buffets. By all accounts, they had a swinging time. Then, a month or so later, they went to a mansion in Rancho Santa Fe, California, and committed mass suicide. Whee! Good times!

Heaven's Gate cult members may have been "beyond human" according to founder Marshall Applewhite, but that didn't stop them from having some out-of-this-world fun in Sin City in the weeks leading up to their communal offing. The cult became infamous when thirty-nine of its members died in an effort to reach a spaceship they believed was trailing Comet Halle-Bop.

In addition to gambling—the group's members won $58.91!—Heaven's Gate members also rode the rides at the Stratosphere (see #202), including one that shot them straight up in the air from the top of the Stratosphere.

Maybe they were hoping to land in that UFO without drinking the metaphorical Kool-Aid!

> " THEY DIDN'T EXACTLY LIVE A LIFE OF DENIAL . . . WE FOUND SEVEN QUARTS OF STARBUCK'S JAVA CHIP ICE CREAM IN THE FREEZER, WHICH IS NOT EXACTLY THE STUFF OF DENIAL. "
> —Susan Jamme, an investigator working on the Heaven's Gate suicide

114. AREA 51

Just ninety miles from Las Vegas is a place where aliens—the outer-space, not the illegal kind—are held prisoner on Earth. Scientists have taken their spacecraft and used them to develop new and top-top-top secret flying machines unlike any our world has ever known.

And if you believe this crap, then get a life.

Area 51 is simply a military base used for the development of new planes and experimental weapons, which explains why the base is off limits to lookie-loos and kooks who have apparently channeled sexual frustration into the development of complex conspiracy theories.

THE TRUE MIDDLE OF NOWHERE

The closest town, if you can call it that, to Area 51 is Rachel, Nevada, which has exactly one business: The Little A'Le'Inn. The Little A'Le'Inn has a bar, some motel rooms, and all the alien-themed crapola you could possibly want.

These theories include—but are sure as hell not limited to—the following: alien autopsies, time travel, teleportation, "shadow" governments (whatever *they* are), and the cryogenically frozen body of Walt Disney. Okay, okay, no one—so far—has suggested that dear old Uncle Walt resides at Area 51, but is that any less difficult to believe than shadow governments?

Our government can't even keep gatecrashers out of the White House. Do you *really* think it could create some ornate, byzantine world of high-tech, alien-engineering and time travel? Scratch Area 51 off your 'must visit' list. You're better off just playing blackjack.

115. FRIEND OF THE ALIENS

Radio Hall of Famer Arthur W. "Art" Bell has built his reputation as the lightning rod for every conspiracy theorist, UFO believer, and pseudoscience proponent in America. As founder and host of the Pahrump, Nevada–based paranormal radio show *Coast to Coast AM*, Bell has held court over the airwaves with such interesting people as:

- ♣ Bugs, a Texas farmer who supposedly shot two Bigfoot animals after mistaking them for bears
- ♣ Oscar, a man purported to be the Son of Satan
- ♣ Victor from Area 51, who claimed responsibility for the infamous three-minute "alien interview" video
- ♣ John Titor, self-styled time traveler and prognosticator purport-edly from 2036

> ❝ I CERTAINLY BELIEVE THAT UFOS ARE REALLY ON OCCASION EXTRA-TERRESTRIAL CRAFT VISITING EARTH, SO TO ME THAT MEANS THAT OUR GOVERNMENT, OUR MILITARY AT SOME LEVEL THEY KNOW THEY'RE HERE, AND THEY'RE EITHER FRIGHTENED OF THEM BECAUSE THEY DON'T KNOW [WHO OR WHAT THEY ARE], OR THEY WISH TO FIGURE A WAY TO DEFEND AGAINST THEM. ❞
>
> —Art Bell

116. RUNNING WITH THE ALIENS

Sure, you can run with the bulls in Pamplona or you can run with Mickey Mouse at Disney World, but only in the State of Nevada can you run with the aliens. Every August the village of Rachel hosts the Extraterrestrial (E.T.) Full Moon Midnight Marathon, Half-Marathon, and 10K—a running event that promises to be out of this world.

The course flanks Area 51 on Highway 375 (officially named the Extraterrestrial Highway by our own U.S. government in 1996)—a stretch of road known for a vast number of purported UFO sightings.

If you're thinking the only place you're running to—in August, in Nevada—is an air-conditioned casino on the Strip, think again. The temperature in Rachel runs 20 degrees cooler than its sister city Las Vegas, and by nightfall, even in the summer, you're talking a sweet 68 degrees.

WATCH OUT FOR EXTRATERRESTRIAL COWS

All participants in the E.T. Full Moon Midnight races are required to wear reflective clothing and a headlamp—or carry a flashlight. Glow necklaces are passed out to all runners as well. This is done to protect you from the potential dangers of the open range. And no, by "dangers" we don't mean extraterrestrials: we mean cows.

You may—or may not—see any aliens on your jog, but the quirky costumes many runners sport, plus the vegetation and vistas of the high desert, are yours to enjoy regardless. And the spread that awaits you at Rachel's Little A'Le'Inn Restaurant will undoubtedly be delicious. You might want to pick up a pair of Alien Head Salt Shakers on your way out.

CHAPTER 12
FRAUDS

117. THE (ALMOST) ANTHRAX ATTACK!

White powder found in Las Vegas? Yawn. It's gotta be coke, right? *What*!? You mean that stuff was *anthrax*!?

Well, sort of. In 1998, a proud member of the Aryan nation named Larry Wayne Harris, was arrested for . . . well, at the time, it wasn't clear exactly *what* he was arrested for. Anyway, he had anthrax. Was he planning to unleash it in Sin City? Was he hatching some other kind of plot? Was he just a "harmless" nutjob racist?

> **MORE ANTHRAX**
> In 2008, Las Vegas experienced another anthrax scare when, at first, authorities believed a dog had been poisoned with the lethal bacteria. The dog turned out to have died from other means.

Reportedly Harris had decided some years before that America needed to defend itself against biological warfare and began exploring all sorts of pseudoscientific methods of inoculating oneself against biological weapons. Gaining (somehow) a nonlethal form of anthrax, Harris claimed he was attempting to use the substance to test equipment that, supposedly, could kill bacteria through sound vibrations or some other such bullshit. Still, he was arrested and later released.

After all, it's no crime to be an Aryan nutjob, especially not in Las Vegas, which welcomes anyone with a quarter for a slot machine.

118. OPERATION G-STING

Do you call it Operation G-Sting? Do you call it Strippergate? And are you *sure* John Edwards and John Ensign weren't involved?

In 2006, seventeen defendants from both Las Vegas and San Diego pleaded guilty to a buffet of offenses related to a lobbyist's efforts to expand strip clubs in San Diego and Sin City. During an FBI probe, dating back to 2001, agents got wind that bribes and unreported "campaign contributions" were being offered to—and accepted by—various Clark County commissioners.

> " DARIO HERRERA IS COMING HOME TO LAS VEGAS, IF YOU CONSIDER A HALFWAY-HOUSE A HOME. "
>
> —Jane Ann Morrison, *Las Vegas Review-Journal*

Allegedly, local strip club owner Michael Galardi wanted to expand his exotic dancing empire from the back roads to the more prestigious Strip. To make certain he would be able to offer full nudity and alcohol—two vices that don't typically mix at Sin City nudie clubs—Galardi spread around some samolians.

The actual sting took place when members of the FBI, DEA, and IRS seized documents from a Galardi property on February 20, 2003. As a result of the subsequent trials, four Clark County commissioners were found guilty of federal corruption charges: Dario Herrera, Erin Kenny, Mary Kincaid-Chauncey, and Lance Malone.

119. ANTOINE WALKER DOESN'T JUST BOUNCE BALLS

From an NBA championship to a trial for bouncing checks to casinos. Tsk, tsk. Walker, who helped lead the Miami Heat to a championship in

2006, has been busy since retiring from the NBA in 2008 . . . racking up tremendous gambling debts at three Las Vegas casinos.

Walker reportedly owes a total of $800,000 to Caesars Palace, Planet Hollywood, and the Red Rock Resort. The power forward pleaded not guilty in June 2010 to charges that he had knowingly written bad checks to these properties to settle his gambling debts.

YOU ARE NOT ALONE

Don't feel bad, Antoine. You're not the only NBA star to have a gambling problem. Wynn Las Vegas filed a civil complaint against Charles Barkley for allegedly failing to pay a $400,000 debt accrued in 2007. Barkley later paid the debt.

Sure, it happens to all of us. Do we have that $135,000 in the bank, or do we just have $135? What's a few zeros, after all? Incidentally, Walker is not just in debt to casinos. When he declared bankruptcy in May 2010, he reported debt to the tune of nearly $13 million.

120. JUDGE HARRY CLAIBORNE VS. THE PIMP

Where else but in Nevada would a brothel owner's testimony topple a federal judge? Well . . . nowhere else, actually.

Harry Claiborne was appointed a federal judge in 1978 by President Jimmy Carter. He was indicted for bribery, fraud, and tax evasion in 1983, resulting in a deadlocked jury. In 1984, he was tried solely for tax evasion, found guilty, and served a prison term in 1986, the year he was impeached and removed from office by the United States House and Senate.

Claiborne was sunk primarily on the testimony of Mustang Ranch owner, Joe Conforte, who claimed he bribed Claiborne to keep the FBI out of his brothel business. So, Sin City has the distinction of having the only federal judge in history convicted of a crime *while serving* in that position.

THE BITTER END FOR CLAIBORNE

Harry Claiborne shot himself to death in 2004, while suffering from Alzheimer's and a host of other health problems.

Many in Las Vegas and in the state of Nevada believed that Claiborne was guilty of nothing more than being fair and impartial toward criminal defendants. Fair and impartial? Where does he think he's practicing law . . . Disneyland?

121. OPERATION YOBO

Named for the misspelling of FBI special agent Joe Yabolonsky (by a Phoenix operative), Operation Yobo became one of Nevada's biggest political scandals. Undercover FBI agent Steve Rybar posed as someone seeking a $15 million loan from Nevada's Public Employees' Retirement System. In order to make sure the voting on the loan went the "right way," he offered cash bribes that were subsequently accepted by five top-ranking state politicians. All five later claimed that they had accepted the money as "consultants" being paid "finder's fees." All five were convicted, although McClelland's case was later overturned due to faulty jury instruction.

Basically, State Senator Floyd Lamb received the largest bribe, $23,000 (and struck a deal to accept $150,000), in the scandal, which broke in 1983. Clark County Commissioner Jack Petitti received $5,000 during an elevator ride. Clark County Commissioner Woodrow Wilson also received $5,000. Reno City Councilman Joe McClelland pocketed $3,750, and State Senator Gene Echols accepted $1,000 *and* requested a word of prayer with Rybar during their meeting.

> " I'M A CHRISTIAN TOO, BUT IT WAS NOT THE RIGHT TIME OR PLACE,
> SO I POOH-POOHED IT. "
>
> —FBI Agent Steve Rybar

Despite this big scandal, politicians in Nevada—like those in most places, come to think of it—don't ever learn from history. Operation G-Sting (see #118) is proof of that.

122. JERRY TARKANIAN: BAD BOY OF BASKETBALL

In 1976, the sports world was shocked, *shocked* we tell you, to find that University of Nevada, Las Vegas (UNLV) head basketball coach Jerry Tarkanian might be guilty of recruiting violations. After all, *no other coach* in the history of college sports has *ever* done anything improper when it comes to recruiting players. The problem with Tark the Shark wasn't that his practices were unusual; it's that he was arrogant about the whole affair.

Tarkanian took the UNLV Runnin' Rebels to the NCAA Final Four a total of four times during his tenure as head coach, from 1973 to 1992, winning the championship in 1990. He's one of the winningest coaches in NCAA history, but he didn't make any effort to hide his questionable recruiting practices. One player, for example, received a "B" in a class he never attended.

The NCAA ordered Tarkanian to be removed in 1976, but the Shark sued and was granted a permanent injunction in 1977, after the Supreme Court agreed that Tarkanian did not receive due process.

Over the years, Tarkanian and the Runnin' Rebels continued to be dogged by scandal, and Tarkanian finally retired in 1992.

> " THERE IS NO ORGANIZATION AS BAD AS THE NCAA. "
>
> —Jerry Tarkanian

123. STARDUST SKIMMING OPERATION

A symbol of the mob's one-time dominance of Sin City was destroyed in 2007 when the venerable (for Las Vegas) Stardust was imploded to make way for Echelon Place (*if* it ever opens).

The Stardust was one of many "classic" casinos operated by the mob, but the goings-on there were the only ones that led to the arrest and conviction of mafia figures for skimming operations.

By the 1970s, the mob's heyday in Las Vegas was over, but that didn't mean the organization wasn't still making money hand over fist. Between 1974 and 1976, the FBI estimated that skimming operations centering on the Stardust earned the mob between $7 million and $15 million.

At the head of the operation was Frank "Lefty" Rosenthal, the Stardust's, um, "entertainment director." At a federal trial in 1985, nine mafia figures said to be part of the skimming operation were convicted or pleaded guilty. Rosenthal was acquitted but banned from casinos for life. He later became the basis of the Robert DeNiro character in Martin Scorsese's *Casino*.

> THERE'S RESIDUAL STUFF . . . BUT THE BIG SHOW IS OVER . . . [THE STARDUST] WAS THE LAST GASP.
>
> —Guy Rocha, Nevada state archivist

124. JOSE VIGOA A.K.A TONY MONTANA?

At age thirteen, Cuban Jose Vigoa was trained by the Soviets to fight in their war with Afghanistan. Vigoa learned how to be a good commando. A few years later, he was part of the Mariel Boatlift—hmm, just like *Scarface's* Tony Montana—a mass exodus from Cuba's Mariel Harbor that brought some 125,000 Cubans to the United States in 1980.

At first, Vigoa tried to make an honest living (so he claims) before he turned to selling coke. Wow! Just like Montana. Vigoa was caught and sent to jail. When released, he set his sights on big-time criminal activity. Using his commando training and analysis of Las Vegas armored car companies, Vigoa robbed five Strip casinos over the course of sixteen months. An attempted robbery of a shopping mall left two guards dead.

> " WE ARE GRATEFUL THAT JOSE VIGOA WILL NEVER WALK THE STREETS OF LAS VEGAS AGAIN. WE JUST HOPE THAT HE DOESN'T HURT SOMEONE IN PRISON. "
>
> —Chief Deputy District Attorney David Roger

A bad disguise and good surveillance cameras helped cops arrest Vigoa after a Bellagio robbery. He will spend the rest of his life in prison. Vigoa makes *Scarface*'s Tony Montana look like a wuss.

125. HUNTING FOR BAMBI IN LAS VEGAS

Forget beer pong. If you're a misogynistic moron looking for more "fun," try Hunting for Bambi. Here's how it goes: Women dressed only in thongs and sneakers run around the Las Vegas desert—personifying Bambis—while men hunt them down and shoot them down with paintball guns. Bambis who manage to avoid getting nailed with paint collect $2,500; those who don't still take home $1,000. Hunters pay $5,000 to $10,000 to blast Bambis.

If you're thinking that this sounds too bizarre to be true, well, you're half right. The *Hunting for Bambi* videos created by Floridian Michael Burdick and sold on *Huntingforbambi.com* turned out to be a hoax: Burdick had hired the women and the hunters and staged the "games."

Hunting for Bambi generated a public outcry, and city officials were quick to issue Burdick a citation for doing business without a license.

But no worries. For all you women-hating creeps out there, *Hunting for Bambi 2* is now on sale on their website.

CHAPTER 13

DISAPPEARING WILDLIFE, JOBS, AND GONZOS

126. ROUND UP TO HELL

Some 37,000 wild horses and burros roam the range on government land in Nevada—including the Las Vegas District. While protected by law from being hunted or killed, when the Bureau of Land Management (BLM) determines that the herds have grown too large, they bring out the helicopters to "gather" whatever burros and horses they can and either move them to holding pens in the Midwest or elsewhere or put them up for adoption. This in effect dooms the wild horses and burros to a life of captivity.

> WE MUST ACT NOW BEFORE THE BLM HAS MANAGED THESE MAGNIFICENT ANIMALS INTO EXTINCTION.
>
> —Willie Nelson

If they even live to be taken captive. "Gathering" mustangs by helicopter is as dangerous as it sounds, and ultimately traumatizes, injures, or kills many of the horses in the process. As for the ones that survive, well, two years ago the BLM proposed a plan to euthanize the excess horses and burros, but shelved that course of action due to public outcry at the time.

But the gatherings still go on. Just last December, horse wranglers hired by the BLM began using helicopters to muster the herds. The plan: to trap at least 2,500 of the wild horses over the next several months. What happens next is anybody's guess. But we're guessing the horses will not be pleased.

127. A WILD HORSE BY ANY OTHER NAME

The wild horses and burros of Nevada are protected by federal law (sort of), but horses that are estrays, feral, or abandoned are not so lucky. They may live in the wild, but that doesn't make them wild—at least not according to the BLM (see #126), an agency apparently not known for its semantic intelligence. And if they're not wild, they often end up in the slaughterhouse.

Here's the logic—to use the term loosely—used by government agencies to define which horses are wild and which ones are feral:

- ♣ **Estray:** a horse living loose in the wild on public land that shows signs of having been domesticated at one time but whose owner, if any, cannot be identified.
- ♣ **Feral:** a horse living loose in the wild on public land that 1) may have once been domesticated but shows no such sign of domestication; or 2) may be the offspring of such an animal.

Wild horses, mustangs, and burros are protected by the 1971 Wild Free Roaming Horses and Burros Act—and as such cannot be sold to the slaughterhouse either directly or indirectly. But, by law, the State of Nevada owns feral, estray, and abandoned horses—and can dispose of them as desired. We're talking dog food or glue.

128. THE WILD HORSE WHISPERERS

Okay, so they're not really wild. At least not according to the BLM (see #126), which rounded up 174 unlucky horses in Pilot Valley, Nevada during the summer of 2010—horses they called feral, estray, and abandoned—and promptly turned them over to the Department of Agriculture for disposal.

Pilot Valley borders the Toano Wild Horse Herd area, where the BLM itself counted 168 wild horses just last year. The BLM has been trying to make the area "horse-free," since 1993—obviously to no avail.

Animal rights activists smelled a rat in this horse business, and questioned the feral designation of the equines. They also questioned the speed to auction—where slaughterhouses from Mexico and Canada typically are the highest bidders—claiming that sufficient time for the notification process and the search for horses' owners required by law had not been given.

HORSE STEW FOR SUPPER!

We may not eat much horse in America, but we slaughter 80,000 horses a year for export to people who do. Horse meat commands as much as $25 a pound in Europe and Asia, where such equine delicacies include horse sashimi in Japan, horse salami in Italy, and horse steak in Belgium. Bon appetit!

Luckily—and with no thanks to the BLM, Department of Agriculture, or the State of Nevada—this is a horse story with a happy ending. Winemaker Ellie Phipps Price of Sand Hill Durell Vineyards in Sonoma, California and Madeleine Pickens, wife of oil magnate T. Boone Pickens, donated the $31,415 needed to outbid the Mexican and Canadian slaughterhouses to win 172 of the 174 horses, according to Lifesavers Wild Horse Rescue. Private citizens bought the other two horses.

129. CITY OF LOST WAGES, INDEED

As recently as 2006, Nevada boasted one of the lowest unemployment rates in the country—only 4.2 percent. Hailed as the new Detroit, Las

Vegas welcomed workers from all backgrounds. You could park cars and make fifty grand a year. And you didn't have to have an education or speak English to do it. No wonder 6,000 people a month moved to Sin City to seek their own version of the American Dream.

Then the bottom fell out; the dream died. In a city so dependent on tourism, the 2008 recession hit especially hard. A bad economy means fewer tourists—and fewer tourists means fewer jobs. By early 2010, Nevada suffered the highest rate of unemployment in America, a whopping 14 percent.

130. TOP JOBS YOU'RE MOST LIKELY TO LOSE IN VEGAS

- ♣ Construction worker
- ♣ Gaming worker
- ♣ Civil servant
- ♣ Educator
- ♣ Legal professional
- ♣ Printing professional
- ♣ Publishing professional

(Source: Nevada Department of Employment, Training and Rehabilitation)

131. TGIF—STARTING AT NOON!

The locals like to say they're just like people everywhere—hardworking, upstanding God-fearing citizens more likely to be found praying at a place of worship in their off-hours than in a gambling establishment. But lame claims that the city boasts more churches per capita than any other city in America aside, we know the locals are full of it. Example: off-strip casinos that cater to locals play a vital role in Sin City's economy.

But perhaps the best proof is in the pools at the Palms. Where else but Vegas could a resort like the Palms establish such a wildly popular event as Ditch Fridays, a poolside bacchanalia that encourages local bros and hos to play hookey every Friday in favor of fun in the sun (and more). Admission is $25—and female natives get in free.

132. WORKING AT A CASINO SUCKS

Casino workers in Las Vegas report lower levels of job satisfaction than non-casino workers, according to the Las Vegas Business Press. Forty million hot, sweaty, drunk, hungry, horny, soon-to-be-broke, loud, and obnoxious nontipping tourists a year . . . What's not to like?

133. FISHING FOR TRANNIES

Unless you're into being transgendered—not that there's anything wrong with that!—don't drink the water in Las Vegas. The water in Sin City comes from Lake Mead, at 9.28 trillion gallons the largest reservoir in the United States. Located on the Colorado River, extending 112 miles behind the Hoover Dam (or the Boulder Dam to locals, see #195), Lake Mead is in both Arizona and Nevada, and both draw upon it for water.

THE THIRST FOR H20

Eight million people in Arizona, Nevada, and California drink water from Lake Mead. As for how many are now hermaphrodites, your guess is as good as ours.

Local authorities claim that the water is fine—but if you really want to know if the water is fine, you should consider the fish that swim in it. And the fish that swim in it are changing.

Male fish in Lake Mead are showing high concentrations of female hormones and are becoming hermaphroditic. They are also full of vitellogenin, a protein previously found only in egg-laying females.

The interesting—if totally disgusting—thing about this is that scientists believe that these abnormal levels are linked to the presence of estrogenic compounds that come not from industrial pollutants but rather from certain substances in women's urine. To be specific: estradiol, estrone, and ethynyl estradiol (found in birth control pills).

Long fish story short: Women pee and male fish go girlie. Go figure.

134. DEAD—AND STINKY—AS A CARP

There's the smell of dead fish, and then there's the smell of dead carp. Last year, thousands of dead carp washed up on the beaches of Lake Mohave, which is part of the Lake Mead National Recreation Area.

YOU CAN BRING A TOURIST TO WATER, BUT . . .

The water in Las Vegas "meets or exceeds" state and federal health standards, according to the Las Vegas Valley Water District. Most of the water used in Las Vegas comes from Lake Mead (ahem).

They looked bad—but they smelled worse. In fact the odor was so offensive that Park officials warned tourists that they may find the fetid perfume of rotting flesh overwhelming—and cautioned against handling the dead carp, as that could conceivably pose a health threat.

Wildlife experts speculated that the fish succumbed to a species-specific virus, as carp were the only fish known to be affected.

This is not the first time the park has seen big carp die-offs; the fish in Lake Mead also suffered a similar fate in 2008, due to low oxygen levels in the water.

Note to reader: This is why you don't drink the water in Las Vegas. Do what the natives do: Stick to gin.

> **IF YOU DAM A RIVER, IT STAGNATES. RUNNING WATER IS BEAUTIFUL WATER.**
>
> —English Proverb

135. THE COLOR OF WATER

There are three colors of water in Las Vegas: clear, grey, and black.

Clear water is the water you drink, that is, the water that comes through the tap from Lake Mead. (If you're thinking about the color of women's urine, see #133 and don't say that we didn't warn you.)

> **A MAN FROM THE WEST WILL FIGHT OVER THREE THINGS: WATER, WOMEN AND GOLD, USUALLY IN THAT ORDER.**
>
> —Barry Goldwater

Grey water is the water from the sinks, bathtubs, and showers of the hotels that is saved, treated, and then used to fill the casinos' manmade waterfalls, fountains, and lakes. (So no matter how tempted you are to frolic in the magnificent Bellagio fountain, think again before you jump in.)

Black water is the water from the toilets, which is piped through to the city sewage system. (Okay, we can hear you sighing in relief.)

136. DON'T DRINK THE WATER

If the hermaphroditic fish don't scare you (see #133), here's another good reason not to drink the water in Las Vegas. According to a recent water quality study in the top 100 municipalities in America, Las Vegas ranks number three on the list of bad water. Only Pensacola, Florida, and Riverside, California scored worse than our little desert oasis. Even more disturbing is the fact that two other Nevada cities also made the Top Ten Worst list—a dubious distinction matched only by the state of California.

And what's in the water that makes it so bad? Toxins like radon, lead, and uranium, all of which have shown up in the local tap water.

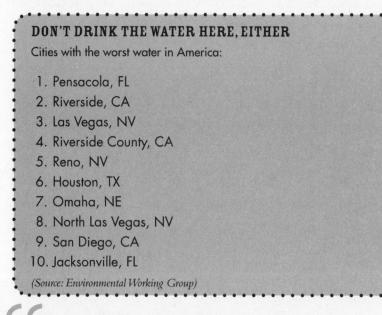

DON'T DRINK THE WATER HERE, EITHER

Cities with the worst water in America:

1. Pensacola, FL
2. Riverside, CA
3. Las Vegas, NV
4. Riverside County, CA
5. Reno, NV
6. Houston, TX
7. Omaha, NE
8. North Las Vegas, NV
9. San Diego, CA
10. Jacksonville, FL

(Source: Environmental Working Group)

> BOTTLED WATER IS NOT REGULATED IN THE SAME WAY AS TAP WATER. WITH BOTTLED WATER, CONSUMERS OFTEN DO NOT KNOW WHAT THEY ARE GETTING, AND 25 TO 40 PERCENT OF BOTTLED WATER ON THE MARKET IS SIMPLY TAP POURED INTO A BOTTLE.
>
> —Olga Naidenko, Environmental Working Group

137. POISON PELLETS OF POOP

Yeah, you read that right. The dreaded quagga mussels have come to Nevada—and with them come their toxic feces, rich in dangerous metals like mercury, selenium, polychlorinated biphenyls (PCBs), and polycyclic aromatic hydrocarbons (PAHs). If that weren't enough, the wretched bivalves make way for the spread of cyanobacteria, a particularly virulent form of algae. The quagga mussels wreaked havoc in the Great Lakes, and their effect on Lake Mead is expected to be far worse, given their preference for warmer waters.

> " IN TERMS OF POTENTIAL ECOLOGICAL IMPACT AND ECONOMIC LOSS, THE QUAGGAS ARE THE WORST THREAT FACING LAS VEGAS. "
> —David Wong, biologist at the University of Nevada, Las Vegas, School of Community Health

Eight million people come to the 1.5-million-acre Lake Mead National Recreation Area every year to swim, boat, fish, water ski, hike, and camp. The contaminants produced by the poop and algae make up a deadly cocktail that pose a real risk to anything—and anyone—in the water. And once the mussels and algae take hold, it's extremely difficult to get rid of them.

138. GERM WARFARE ON THE STRIP

So susceptible is Las Vegas to illness that the U.S. military has chosen UNLV and Las Vegas as the site for a multimillion-dollar research project designed to help protect servicemen and women against epidemics and bioterrorism. Las Vegas is seen as a natural fit for the study, as the travel patterns of tourists in and out of the city are surprisingly similar to those of troops in and out of war zones. During the course of the study, computer models track tourists who are struck by illness and hospitalized during their stay. Such data should help the military track and stop the spread of illness on ships, bases, etc., as well as help ensure that troops do not carry illness back home upon their return from service in other countries.

The research also includes social modeling that identifies where tourists go and who they meet, and the ways in which they are exposed to illness.

> **IT IS ESTIMATED THAT MOST PEOPLE SPEND AS MUCH AS 90 PERCENT OF THEIR TIME INDOORS. INDOOR AIR LEVELS OF MANY POLLUTANTS MAY BE TWO TO FIVE TIMES, AND OCCASIONALLY MORE THAN 100 TIMES, HIGHER THAN OUTDOOR LEVELS.**
>
> —U.S. Environmental Protection Agency

139. CATCHING THE VEGAS COLD

With 40 million tourists from all over the world rubbing elbows, hips, and various other private parts, the exposure to germs is nothing if not high. The odds of catching something—from the common cold to far more serious illnesses—are not necessarily in your favor.

In recent years Las Vegas has suffered outbreaks of the Norovirus, H1N1, hepatitis, salmonella, influenza, and more. Add in dry desert air, secondhand smoke, recirculated air on planes, rich food, alcohol, sleepless nights, the hot days and often surprisingly cool nights, and it's no wonder many tourists live in fear of catching the Vegas Cold.

In fact, repeat visitors swear that precautions should be taken to avoid getting sick every time you hit the Strip. Such tactics include:

- ♣ Antibacterial wipes
- ♣ Nasal spray

- ♣ Drinking lots of fluids
- ♣ Dressing in layers
- ♣ Vitamin C and B12
- ♣ Dietary supplements such as Airborne

140. THE POKER CHIP DISEASE

One of the biggest breeding grounds for germs in Las Vegas is the ubiquitous poker chip. Casinos recognize the risk, and do clean the chips, but
that's no guarantee. According to health studies, one of the most common infections spread from poker chips is Staphylococcus aureus—and
its very dangerous strain, methicillin-resistant Staphylococcus aureus
(MRSA). In the United States alone, some 2.5 million people are car-
riers of MRSA.

> " YOU CAN GET SICK FROM POKER CHIPS. "
>
> —Dr. Charles Stillman, physician and poker player

WASH YOUR HANDS ... AGAIN

The best way to avoid germs is to wash your hands. The trick is to wash
them well enough to actually get rid of the bacteria. The Center for Dis-
ease Control advises people to scrub hands, wrists, and forearms up
to the elbows under running water with an antimicrobial cleanser for
twenty seconds—about as long as it takes to sing "Happy Birthday"
two times.

141. THE DISAPPEARANCE OF DR. GONZO

In 1971, Oscar Zeta Acosta joined the ranks of immortal literary side-kicks: Huck and Jim, Sal Paradise and Dean Moriarty, Dr. Gonzo and Raoul Duke. Then, just two years later, he disappeared without a trace.

Hunter S. Thomspon, a.k.a. Raoul Duke, first met the future Dr. Gonzo, Oscar Zeta Acosta, in 1967. At the time, Thompson was still more "legitimate" reporter than freak-flag-flying gonzo journalist. Acosta was involved with the Chicano Movement.

> OSCAR WAS NOT INTO SERIOUS STREET-FIGHTING, BUT HE WAS HELL ON WHEELS IN A BAR BRAWL.
>
> —Hunter S. Thompson

The two became friends, and Thompson invited Acosta on the trips—to Las Vegas and on LSD—that became the basis of his book *Fear and Loathing in Las Vegas*. Acosta was not, supposedly, pleased that his character was described as a "300-pound Samoan," since Acosta was neither three hundred pounds, nor Samoan.

Just three years after Thompson's book, Acosta disappeared while in Mexico . . . probably at the hands of drug dealers. Acosta was a lawyer and activist, but he also loved his drugs. The body of Dr. Gonzo, Las Vegas companion extraordinaire, has never been found.

142. HOW HOT IS LAS VEGAS REALLY?

Las Vegas is hot. Sunny 85 percent of the time, Las Vegas is so hot that the temperature exceeds 100 degrees Fahrenheit more than seventy days a year. In the summer the temperature can climb as high as 117 degrees—a danger to residents, as well as tourists. In fact, extreme heat kills more people than any other extreme weather except hurricanes, according to the National Weather Service.

> "THE SECRET AFFINITY BETWEEN GAMBLING AND THE DESERT: THE INTENSITY OF GAMBLING REINFORCED BY THE PRESENCE OF THE DESERT ALL AROUND THE TOWN. THE AIR-CONDITIONED FRESH-NESS OF THE GAMING ROOMS, AS AGAINST THE RADIANT HEAT OUTSIDE. THE CHALLENGE OF ALL THE ARTIFICIAL LIGHTS TO THE VIOLENCE OF THE SUN'S RAYS. NIGHT OF GAMBLING SUNLIT ON ALL SIDES; THE GLITTERING DARKNESS OF THESE ROOMS IN THE MIDDLE OF THE DESERT."
>
> —Jean Baudrillard

ONE THIRSTY CITY

Las Vegas is the second driest city in America—and no, we don't mean booze, we mean waterfall. Only Yuma, Arizona is drier—which is why Las Vegas boasts one of the highest consumption rates of Big Gulps. Just ask 7-Eleven. (Source: NOAA)

143. NEVADA TEST SITE

Where else but in Nevada—some sixty miles from Las Vegas, no less—could you find a tourist trap comprised of a place used for nuclear testing? Wait, don't answer. Here's another question: Why do people want to visit this spot in the first place?

Beginning on January 27, 1951, underground nuclear tests began to take place in Frenchman Flat. By 1992, when testing stopped, nearly 1,000 nuclear bombs had been set off from this spot.

The tests made for some mondo-cool photos, such as an iconic one of downtown Las Vegas, in which Vegas Vic (the iconic neon cowboy on Fremont Street) appears to be pointing at a mushroom cloud, but let's back up for a second . . . *They conducted nuclear testing sixty miles from a major resort city!*?

When the Cold War ended, the test site was transformed into a tourist spot. Once a month, folks can go out and tour the remnants of so-called "survivability structures," places built to see how they would survive a nuclear blast.

Interested? Better book now. These tours are hugely popular.

WANT TO GO NUKE-YOU-LAR?

Tours of the Nevada Test Site are administered by the United States Department of Energy. They're free, but they fill up fast. For more information, go to *www.nv.doe.gov/nts/tours.aspx.*

Part Five

WRATH

CHAPTER 14

MOB VIOLENCE

144. BUGSY BITES IT

Bugsy Siegel is often credited with "inventing" the Las Vegas Strip. That's not true. What Bugsy did was add a dash of nouveau riche class to Sin City. Prior to Benjamin "call-me-Bugsy-only-if-you-want-to-die" Siegelbaum's arrival, the Strip only had a couple of low-class Western-themed properties.

Siegel set his sights on creating the Flamingo, a high-class, high-roller resort that would attract the glitterati and quasi-celebrities so rampant in Hollywood. He got his money the old-fashioned way: from the mob. A member of the Genovese crime family, Siegel first arrived in Las Vegas on their behalf. But Bugsy longed to be legit. In 1946, he began the Flamingo project, but then he screwed up big time.

> CLASS, THAT'S THE ONLY THING THAT COUNTS IN LIFE. CLASS. WITH-OUT CLASS AND STYLE, A MAN'S A BUM; HE MIGHT AS WELL BE DEAD.
>
> —Benjamin "Bugsy" Siegel

The mob doesn't like to lose money, and Bugsy's Flamingo became the archetypal money pit and closed soon after it opened in December 1946. That sealed Bugsy's fate.

By the spring of 1947, the Flamingo was reopening, and Siegel's brain-child started to make a profit. But it was too late. On June 20, 1947, Siegel was relaxing at the Los Angeles home of his girlfriend, Virginia Hill, when a hail of bullets crashed through the window, killing him instantly.

145. BUGSY'S BOY: MICKEY COHEN

Born in Brooklyn in 1913, Meyer Harris "Mickey" Cohen was a boxer who did more fighting on behalf of the mob than he ever did in the ring. Mickey started off his career boxing in illegal prize fights, then did a stint as an enforcer with the Chicago mob during Prohibition. Meyer Lansky sent him out West to babysit Bugsy Siegel—where he helped Siegel open the Flamingo Hotel and oversaw the sports betting there. Cohen established the race wire, one of the most successful gambling innovations in Vegas history.

When Bugsy Siegel was murdered by his crime "family," Cohen allegedly went nuts, storming the lobby of the Hotel Roosevelt, where the assassins were supposedly registered, and calling for Bugsy's killers, guns firing.

Cohen ended up doing time in Alcatraz for tax evasion—but he had a good time hobnobbing with the Rat Pack while it lasted. He also did time at the Atlanta Federal Penitentiary. But Cohen had the last laugh, appearing on TV with Merv Griffin and with Billy Graham at rallies in his dotage before dying peacefully in his sleep in 1976.

> **FUCK! LOOK AT ME, FUCK YOU! AND IF I WAS YOU, I'D SHUT MY FUCKIN' MOUTH AND WATCH MY STEP! YEAH, YOU, SMILEY! OR WOULD YA LIKE ME TO BLOW YOUR FUCKIN' ADAM'S APPLE DOWN YOUR SPINE?**
>
> —Harvey Keitel as Mickey Cohen in the Warren Beatty film *Bugsy*

146. SAM GIANCANA: FRANK'S PAL

Benjamin "Bugsy" Siegel was one member of the mob who helped make Vegas Vegas (see #144), but he was not alone. Another member of "the Family" who helped put the "sin" in Sin City was Sam Giancana.

By the 1950s, Giancana was a leader of the powerful Chicago Outfit, which had its fingers in pies throughout the country, including in Las Vegas. Giancana's purview was the Stardust and the Riviera. He became one of those listed in Nevada Gaming Commission's infamous "black book," (see #150) containing names of undesirables (mostly mobsters) who weren't welcome in Nevada casinos.

> **" I STEAL. "**
>
> —Sam Giancana

The stain on Giancana wound up tarring Frank Sinatra as well. Sinatra was part owner of several Nevada properties, including the Sands in Las Vegas and the Cal Neva in Lake Tahoe. When the powers that be figured out that Sinatra allowed his buddy, Giancana, to stay at the Cal Neva, the Chairman of the Board was forced out of the casino business.

Sinatra could hold a grudge like few others, but it isn't likely he had anything to do with Giancana's 1975 murder. *That* was most likely due to the fact that Giancana was doing some work on the side for the CIA.

147. S'LONG, ANTHONY SPILOTRO

You know that crazy guy Joe Pesci played in Martin Scorsese's *Casino*? The one ready to erupt into violence at any time? Well, he was based on Anthony "The Ant" Spilotro, a real-life crazy mobster.

Spilotro became the Chicago Outfit's Las Vegas enforcer in 1971. After casino profits were tallied, Spilotro and partner Frank "Lefty" Rosenthal skimmed a good portion off the top for their Chicago bosses.

Spilotro's job was to make sure no casino employees tried to toy with the mob's profits. Being a scary guy, Spilotro was very successful at his enforcing job. He also, ironically, found the time to run the gift shop at Circus Circus, the Strip's first family-oriented casino.

In 1986, Spilotro, believing he was about to be asked to join "the family," was killed in Indiana and buried in a cornfield. For years, it was believed he was buried alive, but most likely, Spilotro was already dead when he was put in the ground.

> " WHEN IT LOOKED LIKE THEY COULD GET TWENTY-FIVE YEARS TO LIFE IN PRISON JUST FOR SKIMMING A CASINO, SICK OR NO FUCKIN' SICK, YOU KNEW PEOPLE WERE GOING TO GET CLIPPED. "
>
> —Joe Pesci as Nick Santoro, a character based on Anthony Spilotro,
> in *Casino*

148. DON'T MESS WITH "FAT HERBIE"

You would have to be superhumanly scary to serve as muscle for Tony "The Ant" Spilotro (see #147), who was *really* scary. But the workaholic mobster Herbert "Fat Herbie" Blitzstein didn't stop there! He also found time to be a charter member of the Hole in the Wall Gang.

THAT'S NOT HOW IT HAPPENED
In *Casino*, the character based on Blitzstein was killed by Las Vegas police during a bungled robbery.

The Hole in the Wall Gang operated out of the not-at-all legit Gold Rush Jewelry Store in Sin City. The gang got its name because, in an effort to stock the jewelry store, it would punch "holes in the wall" of other establishments and steal their stuff.

Fat Herbie was lucky. When members of the gang were caught breaking into a business on July 4, 1981, Blitzstein wasn't with them. When he and Spilotro were later brought up on racketeering charges, those charges were dropped for insufficient evidence.

But Fat Herbie's luck—as it does for most Las Vegas gamblers—ran out in January 1997 when he was shot gangland style by some former "associates."

149. MOB MAYOR: OSCAR GOODMAN

Look up the words "outspoken" and "unapologetic" in your dictionary, and you'll find them illustrated with a picture of His Honor, Oscar Goodman, Las Vegas's mayor since 1999.

Goodman made his name by defending a number of mafia figures who passed through Sin City: Meyer Lansky, Nicky Scarfo, Herbert "Fat Herbie" Blitzstein (see #49), Frank "Lefty" Rosenthal, and Tony "The Ant" Spilotro (see #147), among them.

A background defending notable mob figures might preclude someone from entering politics in most cities, but in Las Vegas, Goodman's (in)famous resume has made him one of the most popular mayors Sin City has ever seen. Still, he gets into trouble now and then (remember what he told those fourth graders he'd take to a desert island?).

(Un)fortunately, Goodman began serving his last term in 2007. City term limits won't allow for a fourth term in office.

150. THE STATE'S LITTLE BLACK BOOK

A city smack dab in the middle of the desert would still just be a whistle stop if it weren't for such figures as Benjamin Siegel and Moe Dalitz. So why would Nevada's Gaming Comission create the so-called "black book," filled with people—many of them mobsters—not allowed to even step onto casino property?

Self-preservation!

In 1960, the Gaming Control Board created a list—originally with eleven names—of notorious mobsters who had to stay out of casinos in order to prevent the government from regulating-to-death the state's main source of revenue. As Las Vegas gained more attention nationally, the government started sniffing around, not eager to give tacit approval to an industry that seemed built on a house of "made" men. So, the state began to police itself.

WHO'S IN YOUR LITTLE BLACK BOOK?

Past and present "honorees" in the Nevada Gaming Commission's "black book" include mob-related figures Frank Rosenthal, James Tamer, Anthony St. Laurent, and Charles Panarella. Run-of-the-mill cheaters in the book include Douglas William Barr, Michael Joseph Balsamo, William Land, and Timothy Childs.

Eventually, the book, nicknamed the "black book" because the people on it are "blacklisted," also gained the names of known cheaters. At present, the book is around forty pages long.

151. A DIFFERENT KIND OF MOB: THE RODNEY KING AFTERMATH

Most Sin City tourists never go North of Glitter Gulch, and with good reason. The northern part of the city is crime-ridden and offers textbook examples of urban blight. In the spring of 1992, North Las Vegas wasn't just a breeding ground for petty theft and burglary, it became a hotbed of rioting.

Why? Well, do you remember Rodney King? The guy who cops beat the crap out of—on tape—in Los Angeles? Do you remember that many folks in poor, largely African-American portions of LA went totally apeshit when the police officers were acquitted of all wrongdoing on April 29, 1992? The same thing happened in Las Vegas after the Rodney King verdict was read.

> CAN WE ALL. . . JUST. . . GET ALONG?
>
> —Rodney King

For a month following the officers' acquittal, North Las Vegas erupted in rioting and mob violence. Stores were looted. Buildings, including the local chapter of the NAACP, were burned. Snipers shot at passing police cars. And one man, Karel Kuthan, was pulled from his car and nearly beaten to death while on his way to his job as a security guard.

So, what happens in Vegas may stay in Vegas, but when shit goes down in LA, it spreads like wildfire in the Santa Ana winds.

CHAPTER 15

HOMICIDE

152. THE DEATH OF KATHY AUGUSTINE

Nevada's first female state controller (a sort of state accountant) and a finalist for Treasurer of the United States, was killed in 2006 allegedly by her fourth husband, a male nurse named William Charles "Chaz" Higgs. The moral of the story: Never trust a guy named Chaz, and if the third time's no charm, then marriage just may not be for you.

Kathy Augustine served as a Nevada state senator before she became controller in 1998. She was not above dirty tricks. Augustine claimed, for example, that her senatorial opponent refused to stand for the Pledge of Allegiance when, in fact, the Jewish man simply declined to take part in a prayer by a Christian minister.

Augustine's death came in the midst of her campaign for state treasurer. At first, authorities believed Augustine died from a heart attack. Then, after telltale traces of a paralyzing drug were found in her system, Chaz attempted suicide in the couple's Las Vegas home. He remains in prison and on suicide watch.

> SHE KNEW THAT HER JUDGMENT IN MEN WAS FLAWED. KATHY WAS LOUSY ON RELATIONSHIPS. SHE WAS GREAT AT POLITICS, BUT NOT GOOD THE OTHER WAY.
>
> —Heidi Smith, longtime Augustine friend

153. THE MURDER OF LITTLE SHERRICE

A seven-year-old girl, a careless parent, and a child-pornography-viewing sleaze ball all found themselves in a casino near Las Vegas back in 1997. The result was the death of Sherrice Iverson, the imprisonment of sleaze ball Jeremy Strohmeyer, and beefed-up security in casinos.

Strohmeyer, eighteen, was in the Primadonna Casino, on the Nevada-California border on May 25, 1997, with his buddy, David Cash—a University of California, Berkeley student—and Cash's father. Iverson's father was really busy with the important activity of gambling and allowed his daughter to run around the casino unaccompanied.

> I JUST WANTED TO EXPERIENCE DEATH.
>
> —Jeremy Strohmeyer

Strohmeyer began to "play" with the girl, ultimately taking her into one of the casino's bathrooms, where he proceeded to rape and strangle her. At one point, Cash walked in, saw what was going on, and left without telling the resort's security what he had seen.

Of course, one wonders why the dad's priorities were so off and why security was so lax to begin with, but that would change . . . after it was too late for Iverson. Another result of her death was the so-called Sherrice Iverson Bill, which made it a crime for folks to see a child being molested and remain silent like Cash did.

154. TUPAC SHAKUR

For many, rap artist and actor Tupac Shakur was more than just a gangsta rapper who liked to opine about bitches and hos. The charismatic artist represented East Coast rap, and his social activism made him akin to a hip-hop John Lennon.

Unfortunately, like Lennon, Shakur's life also ended tragically. Shakur was shot multiple times on September 7, 1996, near the intersection of Flamingo Avenue and Koval Lane in Las Vegas. He died a week later.

Shakur's death practically matches JFK's in terms of the number of conspiracies surrounding it. Was Tupac killed due to an East Coast/West Coast rap rivalry? Did Death Row Records magnate Suge Knight have something to do with Shakur's death? Was the subsequent murder of the Notorious B.I.G. a response to Shakur's death? To date, no one has ever been arrested in connection with Shakur's death.

155. UP IN SMOKE

After Shakur's body was cremated, some of his ashes were mixed with marijuana and smoked by members of the Outlawz, a New Jersey–based rap group founded by Shakur. Hey, don't bogart that Tupac, my friend.

> " MY MAMA ALWAYS USED TO TELL ME: IF YOU CAN'T FIND SOMETHIN' TO LIVE FOR, YOU BEST FIND SOMETHIN' TO DIE FOR. "
> —Tupac Shakur

156. BUFORD FURROW

Las Vegas attracts people who act crazy, so it stands to reason that it also attracts crazy people. Case in point: Buford Furrow.

In case you've forgotten, he's the former member of the Aryan Nation who shot up a Jewish day care in the summer of 1999 in Los Angeles. The shooting injured three small children. Later that same day, not content with merely being an anti-Semite, Furrow shot and killed a Filipino American mailman.

Furrow lived throughout California and Washington before he committed his hate crimes, but when it came time to surrender to police, he knew there was only one perfect place to do it: Sin City. Vegas, baby! He turned himself in to authorities in August of 1999.

> **MY MIND WAS FILLED WITH SICKNESS AND UNFORTUNATELY I ACTED ON IT. BUT NOW I'M A MODEL PRISONER . . . AND MY FUTURE WILL NEVER INCLUDE NEO-NAZI ACTIVITY AGAIN.**
> —Buford Furrow

Furrow is currently serving a life sentence in an Indiana prison, but in a "heartwarming" development, he claims he has renounced his earlier racist views. How come it takes some people being imprisoned before they find Jesus? For most Las Vegas visitors, all it takes is a lucky turn at the craps table.

157. 9/11 HIJACKERS DO VEGAS

Just before they took part in the worst act of terrorism committed on American soil, five of the 9/11 hijackers engaged in some activities of which Allah would not approve. Where did they decide to go to drink, gamble, and ogle strippers? Vegas. Duh.

Marwan al-Shehhi, Mohammed Atta, and others met up in Sin City just weeks before they flew planes into the World Trade Center, the Pentagon, and crashed into a Pennsylvania field. Authorities were baffled. Some had also gone to Vegas as many as six times in the months leading up to 9/11. *Why* had they gone to Las Vegas?

For the same reason *everyone* goes to Vegas, you chowderheads. Didn't we just mention that they were there to drink, gamble, and ogle strippers?

They spent some time at the Olympic Garden Topless Cabaret. A few of the guys stayed at Circus Circus and hung out at a local Starbucks.

Most likely, the guys just wanted to, you know, let it all hang out before they committed acts of "self-sacrifice" that would send them to a land filled with virgins . . . something Vegas definitely is *not*.

> **I'M GLAD HE'S DEAD WITH THE REST OF THEM, AND I DON'T LIKE FEELING SOMETHING LIKE THAT. BUT HE WASN'T JUST A BAD TIPPER—HE KILLED PEOPLE.**
>
> —Olympic Garden dancer, referring to one of the terrorists, as quoted
>
> on *sfgate.com*

158. SANDY AND TED'S EXCELLENT ADVENTURE

Buried treasure. A Topless dancer turned (alleged then acquitted) murderer. Drug addiction and the loss of a casino empire. Ted Binion: This was your life!

Ted Binion was the son of Benny Binion, owner of Binion's Horseshoe. After the old man was convicted of (among other things) tax evasion, Ted and his brother took over operation of the famous casino.

Fast forward many years. Ted Binion got himself into all sorts of trouble due to drug abuse, coziness with mobsters, etc. During this period, he found himself a much younger girlfriend, stripper Sandy Murphy.

When Binion lost his gaming license, he managed to transfer six tons of silver bullion from the Horseshoe's vault to a secret vault he had dug into the Nevada desert near Pahrump. But Binion became increasingly despondent and killed himself on September 17, 1998.

Or did he? Murphy and her married lover, Rick Tabish, were put on trial for Binion's death. They were convicted, the conviction was overturned on technicalities, they were put on trial again, and this time they were acquitted of Binion's murder.

> **I'VE HAD SO MANY THINGS SAID ABOUT ME IN THE LAST YEAR AND A HALF, MOST OF THE TIME I LAUGH.**
>
> —Sandy Murphy

159. THE REAL (DICKWEED) MCCOY

Las Vegas is a freak magnet. Just look at the sad, pathetic life of Charles McCoy, Jr.

In case you've forgotten him, McCoy is the guy accused of twenty-four shootings that took place on and around Columbus, Ohio freeways between May 2003 and March 2004. The shootings resulted in the death of Gail Kinsey who was on the freeway en route to a doctor's appointment.

As the net tightened around McCoy, he disappeared. His loved ones put out a desperate plea for him to give himself up.

> **I'M SORRY FOR NOT TAKING MY MEDICATION AND PUTTING YOU AND EVERYONE THROUGH THIS.**
>
> —Charles McCoy, Jr.

McCoy was found—you guessed it—in Sin City.

McCoy's 2005 trial resulted in a hung jury. After all, this guy was certifiable, diagnosed in 1996 with paranoid schizophrenia. Instead of a retrial, McCoy accepted a plea bargain that put him in jail for twenty-seven years.

So . . . what happened outside of Vegas, went to Vegas, left Vegas, and wound up in prison somewhere. Whatever happened to just going to Vegas for the buffets?

160. NEW YORK NEW YORK SHOOTING

Nothing closes down a Las Vegas casino. *Nothing.* Not even some madman shooting indiscriminately at people who are just trying to get some money without working for it.

> **THAT'S WHAT AMAZED ME. THEY LOCKED DOWN THE TABLES, BUT THEY LET PEOPLE STILL KEEP PLAYING THE SLOTS.**
>
> —Larry Ramos, bystander

Before Hungarian immigrant Steven Zegrean went over-the-top nuts, he had been just run-of-the-mill nuts, threatening various family members with bodily harm. But in July 2007, he allegedly shot sixteen rounds onto the floor of the New York New York casino, leaving four people wounded. The incident was remarkable for several reasons. First of all, one tends to think of Las Vegas casinos as among the safest place on the planet, due to intense security. Secondly, Zegrean was not apprehended by casino security but by off-duty armed services personnel. Thirdly, no one (thankfully) was killed, despite the casino being pretty packed.

But the most amazing aspect of the crime is that folks went right on gambling through it. The tables were closed temporarily, but little old ladies kept pulling those slot arms without a second glance. Maybe their hearing aids were off?

161. THE LUXOR BOMBS

A pipe bomb disguised as a cup of overpriced coffee. Sounds like something from *24*, doesn't it? But on May 7, 2007, just such a device killed one man atop the Luxor's parking garage.

Porfirio Duarte-Herrara was convicted of making the sophisticated weapon that killed Willebaldo Dorantes Antonio. Dorantes Antonio's girlfriend, Caren Chali, was not injured in the incident. When Dorantes Antonio picked up the wired coffee cup, it sent shrapnel ripping through his hand and into his brain.

> **THE DEVICE AND THE WAY IT WAS MANUFACTURED AND DETONATED IN THIS CASE SHOWS A CONSCIOUS DESIRE FOR IT TO BE VICTIM-INITIATED AND FOR IT TO BE LETHAL.**
> —David Stanton, prosecutor

The motive? Who the hell knows? Maybe jealousy. Maybe some anonymous score. Maybe Duarte-Herrara is just a wacko who likes to make bombs and kill people with them. He also is believed to have set off a bomb, which did not kill or injure anyone, in a Home Depot parking lot.

Home Depot should have given the guy an endorsement deal for demonstrating the success of do-it-yourself projects. Instead, Duarte-Herrara earned life in prison without parole.

162. JOHN MATTHUS WATSON III: THE TEACHING CANNIBAL

Apparently, California math teacher John Matthus Watson III was upset with the dining choices offered by Tuscany Suites and Casino, an off-the-Strip spot. Therefore, he resorted to cannibalism. There. It's just that simple.

> **I STIPULATE TO [THE DEATH PENALTY]. I AGREE.**
> —John Matthus Watson III

In 2006, Watson took his wife, Everilda, to the Tuscany to celebrate her fiftieth birthday. The former math teacher's idea of a celebration was to kill and dismember the mother of three, then cook part of her body and eat it.

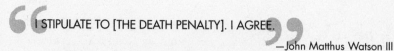

Actually, the motive seems to be money. Somehow, Watson had managed to save a million dollars (did we mention he was a *math teacher?*). When his wife began to talk of leaving him and taking half his money, Watson went out and bought a band saw.

Watson was sentenced to death in June 2010 for the murder. In fact, he requested a death sentence. Watson converted to Islam while in prison and felt that death was the only proper punishment for his crime. Well, you got your wish, Mr. Watson.

163. SERIAL MURDERER IN SIN CITY?

In 2008, America's Most Wanted suggested that a serial killer was loose in Sin City, killing prostitutes. Yes, we know what you're thinking. Prostitution is illegal in Las Vegas, so how, *how* could this happen? Well, some folks, apparently, break the law and buy nightly companionship. And, just maybe, one of them also is a killer.

> **I BELIEVE WHATEVER HAPPENED TO LINDSAY, WHATEVER HAPPENED TO JESSIE . . . THIS IS NOT THE FIRST TIME THEY HAVE DONE IT, AND THEY ABSOLUTELY KNOW HOW TO GET AWAY WITH IT.**
>
> —Bob Harris, Lindsay Harris's father

Between 2003 and 2006 four known prostitutes disappeared from Las Vegas. One of them, Jessie Foster, has never been found. Another, Jodi Brewer, disappeared in 2003. Friends and family searched for her for two weeks before her remains were found in northern California. When remains were found in the desert near Las Vegas in 2003, it took two years to figure out they belonged to the third missing prostitute, Misty Saens. In 2005, police near Springfield, Illinois, discovered a severed pair of women's legs. DNA testing proved that the appendages belonged to Lindsay Harris, the fourth prostitute who had disappeared from Las Vegas.

164. LAUGHLIN RIVER RUN RIOT

They used guns. They used knives. They even used hammers. These men meant business. It was the deadliest event on the floor of a casino in modern Nevada history, and it happened just ninety miles from Sin City, in Laughlin.

A Harley-Davidson dealer started the Laughlin River Run in 1983, and the event has grown larger year by year. In 2002, rival motorcycle gangs sparked an incident known as the River Run Riot.

> WE KNOW OF NOTHING OF THIS MAGNITUDE HAPPENING INSIDE A CASINO IN THE HISTORY OF GAMBLING SINCE 1931, WHEN GAMBLING WAS LEGALIZED IN NEVADA. THIS IS SOMETHING VERY NEW ON THE LANDSCAPE.
>
> —Guy Rocha, Nevada state archivist

Members of the Hell's Angels and the Mongols motorcycle clubs began to attack each other inside Harrah's Hotel & Casino in Laughlin. When the dust settled, three men were dead. Anthony Barrera, a Mongol, was stabbed to death. Jeramie Bell and Robert Tumelty, both Hell's Angels, were shot to death. Apparently, no one died from hammer blows, though that would have made the brawl legendary. It was, however, the first time a multiple homicide took place inside a Nevada casino. Six members of each gang were convicted and sent to prison for the riot.

165. KILLED IN A CASINO

Latrovia Reed's murder of "Lil Angel" marks the most recent murder to take place on the floor of a Las Vegas casino . . . supposedly one of the safest spots anywhere.

On September 5, 2008, while preparing to "go to work" at Bally's Casino, Reed and Taleasha "Lil Angel" Jamerson got into a bit of a squabble regarding their pimp. Reed stabbed Jamerson in the neck and ran out of the hotel's lobby. She later pleaded guilty to the crime.

The *first* murder to take place on the floor of a Las Vegas casino occurred in November 1999 when Larry Darnell Taylor shot and killed his ex-girlfriend, Gloria Cohns, as she was dealing blackjack at Glitter Gulch's Golden Gate Casino.

In February 2000, Anthony Cuccia shot and killed Philip Greenspan at the Stardust sports book. The motive? Cuccia believed Greenspan was a mafia hit man sent to kill him. Yes. Cuccia is nuts.

In September 2000, Stephen Mullen shot at security officers inside Harrah's Casino. A stray bullet struck and killed twenty-nine-year-old Heather Vitarelli. Now *that's* the textbook definition of rotten luck in a casino.

> I LAUGHED LIKE A BASTARD [WHEN I SHOT GREENSPAN]. IT WAS COMICAL TO ME.
>
> —Anthony Cuccia

166. THREE'S A CROWD MURDER

Big muscles, little brains. Oh, and little conscience, too. That's the story, in a nutshell, of professional body builders Craig Titus and Kelly Ryan, and their assistant Melissa James.

In December 2005, James was found in the trunk of Ryan's Jaguar, which, by the way, was on fire at the time. Ryan and Titus, one-time International Federation of BodyBuilders competitors, claimed they had fired James just before her burnt corpse was found.

The couple said James had embezzled from them. That's why she was fired. They also said that James had stolen Ryan's car. However, Titus and Ryan had not reported the embezzlement or the stolen car to police. Little brain oversight.

> " I WAS SHOCKED. I NEVER IMAGINED THEY'D BE CAPABLE OF DOING ANYTHING LIKE THIS. "
>
> —Maura James, Melissa James's mother

The apparent motive: jealousy. Titus and James had been having an affair. Possibly, James was using this to get extra favors from her employers. Who knows? The bottom line is that she was murdered and dumped into the trunk of a car that was subsequently set on fire.

Titus and Ryan protested their innocence and went into hiding. On May 31, 2008, the couple returned and surrendered.

167. THE BODYGUARD

Johnny Stompanato was a Marine from Illinois who served in the Pacific and then came home to spend his time working for the mob and bedding beautiful actresses. He was married at least three times, the first time to a Turkish woman he met in China after the war. After leaving her and their son in Illinois, Stompanato, also known as "Handsome Harry," went West to seek his fortune, where he married actress Helen Gilbert—of *The Secret of Dr. Kildare* fame—in Las Vegas in 1949; she was ten years his senior and had been married four times previously. She claimed to grow tired of supporting him and divorced him five months later. Johnny then married another actress—Helene Stanley of *The Snows of Kilimanjaro*—in 1953. That marriage also didn't last, and Johnny took up with a number of other women, including Ava Gardner and Lana Turner.

By all accounts, Johnny was a violent and possessive lover. Which is hardly surprising since his day job—and Johnny's most notorious affiliation—was with his bro Mickey Cohen, for whom he served as bodyguard and moneyman.

While involved with Turner, Johnny confronted her *Another Time, Another Place* leading man Sean Connery on location in the United Kingdom—and the actor humiliated Johnny by taking his unlicensed gun away from him and kicking him off the set. The UK deported him, and he went home pissed.

Back home, the Turner-Stompanato household was not a happy one. Cheryl Crane, Turner's fourteen-year-old daughter stabbed Johnny to death in 1958 in an attempt to protect her mother from her violent lover. The death was ruled justifiable homicide—but rumors that Turner herself stabbed the former Marine persist to this day. Some mobsters blamed Connery, who supposedly had to lay low for awhile.

EPILOGUE

Cohen buried his pal Johnny in a cheap coffin, underwrote the Stompanato family's $7 million lawsuit against the Turners, and handed over Lana Turner's love letters to Johnny to the media—for a price.

168. WHERE THE BODIES ARE BURIED

The hundreds of miles of Mohave Desert that surround the manmade oasis that is Las Vegas are home to the mortal remains of untold numbers of mobsters—and enemies of mobsters. The scorched land here is as unforgiving an environment as the world of organized crime—and in that respect perhaps an appropriate resting place for many of the occupants of the unmarked desert graves.

In the heyday of the mob in Las Vegas, those who died as a result of "heavy work" were handed over to the so-called Hobo Mafia, who commanded high fees to "dig holes" in the desert far beyond the Strip, the better to keep the tourists fat, happy, and ignorant of the violent underworld that really ran the city. Legend has it that the worst offenders were buried with one hand sticking out of the sand as a warning to others who might offend the mob.

> A LOT OF HOLES IN THE DESERT, AND A LOT OF PROBLEMS ARE BURIED IN THOSE HOLES. BUT YOU GOTTA DO IT RIGHT. I MEAN, YOU GOTTA HAVE THE HOLE ALREADY DUG BEFORE YOU SHOW UP WITH A PACKAGE IN THE TRUNK. OTHERWISE, YOU'RE TALKING ABOUT A HALF-HOUR TO FORTY-FIVE MINUTES WORTH OF DIGGING. AND WHO KNOWS WHO'S GONNA COME ALONG IN THAT TIME? PRETTY SOON, YOU GOTTA DIG A FEW MORE HOLES. YOU COULD BE THERE ALL FUCKIN' NIGHT.
>
> —Joe Pesci as Nicky Santoro in *Casino*

CHAPTER 16

ASSAULT

169. THE LEGEND OF MIKE TYSON

Las Vegas resident Mike Tyson isn't just an ear-biter. He's also a convicted rapist. If you'd forgotten that part of Tyson's illustrious curriculum vitae, then that's excusable. After all, he *was* funny as hell in *The Hangover*.

But back to his sordid past. On July 19, 1991, Tyson invited Miss Black Rhode Island Desiree Washington to a party. When Tyson picked up Washington, he began making sexual advances toward her while still in his limo.

> **I'M NOT MOTHER TERESA. BUT I'M ALSO NOT CHARLES MANSON!**
> —Mike Tyson

When they got to Tyson's hotel room, Tyson allegedly forced himself on Washington and raped her. At his trial, the defense argued that Washington was just a gold-digging publicity hound. The real victim? Mike Tyson, of course.

But during cross-examination, Tyson acted like a thug, showing no remorse or even pretending to show any remorse. His performance probably poisoned the jury against him. Tyson was found guilty in 1992 and served three years, which gave him two years to gain an appetite for human flesh, such as Evander Holyfield's ear.

170. THE COMEUPPANCE OF SCOTT SCHWARTZ

Rapists are evil assholes who commit unconscionable acts, but that doesn't mean they're idiots ... except in the case of one-time University of Nevada, Las Vegas honor student Scott Schwartz.

On April 11, 1996, Schwartz attacked and attempted to rape a woman in her East Charleston Boulevard apartment. That's plain evil. But here's why he was also stupid.

> WE KNOW RIGHT NOW, TONIGHT, THAT EVERYONE CAN GO TO SLEEP KNOWING SCOTT SCHWARTZ IS IN PRISON.
> —District Attorney Abbi Silver

While being held at knifepoint, Schwartz's victim offered to perform oral sex on him. When he agreed, she damn near bit off her would-be rapist's schlong. Schwartz ran out of the apartment and drove off ... around the corner to his assigned parking space.

Yep, that's right. He lived in the same apartment complex as the victim. A neighbor saw Schwartz jump into his car, drive off, and then spotted the car in its assigned space.

When police arrived, they got a look at the mangled penis, which pretty much made the attempted-rape case a slam dunk for the prosecution.

Maybe he wasn't a complete and total idiot. At least he found time during all of this to get his degree in hotel management from UNLV.

171. FIRE ON THE MOUNTAIN: MT. CHARLESTON EVACUATIONS

God doesn't just strike down casinos like the Palace Station (see #6). He also shows His lack of approval for Sin City by attacking nearby ski resorts.

Yes, that's right. Las Vegas, Sin—and Sun!!—City has a ski resort just down the street from it. Even in the spring, one can see a dusting of snow atop nearby Mt. Charleston. But in the summer of 2010, the awe-inspiring sight was fire.

A wildfire, probably set by an arsonist, broke out on July 1, quickly gobbling up thirteen acres and coming within a thousand feet of local homes and campsites before being contained.

> " THE WINDS ARE SWIRLING, AND IT'S ABOUT A MILE FROM MY HOUSE. IRONICALLY, THIS FIRE IS ON THE ANNIVERSARY OF THE ONE THAT WAS STARTED BY THAT PLANE CRASH. "
>
> —Jim Laurie, Mt. Charleston resident

No one was injured in the fire, which marked the *second* time Mt. Charleston had to be evacuated for a blaze. Two years earlier, a private plane crashed in the area, causing a fire that burned through twelve acres.

Hey, Earth to God: The gambling's not on Mt. Charleston. Go after the casinos, Your Excellency. The *casinos*.

172. THE MGM GRAND FIRE

On November 21, 1980, the MGM Grand became twenty-six stories of death when a fire broke out in the kitchen of one of the MGM Grand's restaurants (it's now the site of Bally's). Within moments, a fireball swept through the main casino, killing some who had little to no advance notice of anything amiss. Most people died in the stairwells and on the upper floors of the building because the hotel tower's design effectively turned the "emergency stairs" into giant chimneys that drew up toxic smoke.

Sprinklers? What sprinklers? The state's building inspectors granted the MGM an exemption from them because—get this—the property was in use twenty-four hours a day. So, you know, folks could easily inform others of a fire.

When it was all over, eighty-four people had lost their lives. Only a 1946 fire in Atlanta's Winecoff Hotel was worse (119 died in that blaze). Not long after the fire, MGM sold the property to Bally's.

> DOES IT SURPRISE ANYONE THAT THERE ARE MORE SAFEGUARDS TAKEN TO PROTECT THE GLITTERING MARQUEES OUT FRONT THAN THE LIVES OF THOSE WHO WILL BE HOUSED INSIDE THESE HOTELS?
>
> —Tom Fitzpatrick, *Arizona Republic Reporter*

Oh, and after all those people died, and one more fatal fire (see #173), safety codes became stricter.

173. THE LAS VEGAS HILTON FIRE

Just ninety days after the MGM Grand fire killed eighty-four people, another deadly fire broke out in Las Vegas. Firefighters responded on February 10, 1981 to a report of a fire at the Las Vegas Hilton. Flames were twenty-two stories high. You don't hear much about this one because it "only" killed eight people.

> THIS IS THE LAST HAND, AND I DO MEAN THE LAST HAND.
>
> —Las Vegas Hilton security guard, prior to sending gamblers out of the casino

Before you say, "Why didn't they learn from the MGM fire?" keep in mind that the property (still the world's largest Hilton hotel) was in the midst of being retrofitted with up-to-date safety equipment at the time of the fire. In addition, this hotel fire was not an accident. It was started by a fourteen-karat douchebag named Phillip Bruce Cline.

Cline was working as a room service busboy when the fire broke out. At first, he appeared to be a hero. He ran up and down the halls, banging on doors to alert guests about the fire. Investigators quickly realized that Cline was not a hero. He had set fires in four different spots. He remains in the Nevada State Prison.

174. THE MONTE CARLO FIRE

The Monte Carlo is an "overrun" casino. It's not a top-shelf place like the Bellagio, the Venetian, or the MGM Grand (which owns the property). It's one of the spots you go to when those resorts are all booked up. But things got pretty hot at the Monte Carlo on January 25, 2008.

Welders working to set up window-washing equipment on the roof of the casino's tower started a fire that quickly spread to the top six floors of the building. Fortunately for folks on those six floors, the fire was contained to the *outside* of the building. No deaths occurred, though thirteen people suffered from smoke inhalation.

> "THERE WERE A COUPLE OF LADIES CRYING, BUT IT WAS PRETTY CALM."
> —Larry Wappel, Monte Carlo guest

After the smoke cleared, an investigation determined that the fire occurred due to negligence. Union Erectors LLC, it turned out, had not applied for a permit to do the welding work on the roof. In addition, fire protection mats that would have kept sparks from setting ablaze were not used. Cutting corners: the American Way!

175. THE CRAZY HORSE TOO BEATINGS

Fair warning: Don't start any shit in Las Vegas strip clubs, or you may end up like Interstate trucker Scott Fau, who got into a fight with bouncers at Crazy Horse Too in the summer of 1995. Police were called to the scene to break it up. Three hours after Fau left the scene, he was found with serious injuries that had *not* taken place during the original fight. Thirty minutes after the fight at the club, the bouncers wound up at a Las Vegas hospital with minor injuries.

> " HE WASN'T SORRY ONE BIT. "
> —Kirk Henry, speaking of Crazy Horse Too shift manager Bobby D'Apice

Camille Fau alleged that the bouncers followed her husband, continued beating the shit out of him, and left him for dead. Jurors disagreed, saying they did not believe that there was enough time for the bouncers to beat Fau to death before going to the hospital. The Crazy Horse Too bouncers were acquitted.

In 2001, computer cable salesman Kirk Henry got into a dispute at the Crazy Horse Too over an $80 bar tab. He was beaten so severely that his neck was broken, leaving him a quadriplegic. This time, the club and its owner were found liable for the attack and forced to pay Henry $10 million.

176. SUICIDE IS PAINLESS . . . IN LAS VEGAS

Las Vegas is the Suicide Capital of America because suicide rates here are double that of the rest of the country. According to a Harvard University study, if you live in Vegas, the odds of you taking your own life soar; visit Vegas and the odds of your taking your own life soar even higher. What is it about Sin City that encourages people to commit the mortal sin of hastening their own mortality? Here are a few of the theories:

- ♣ Vegas is a boom (or bust) town of transients, where putting down roots is not easy.
- ♣ People without a history of gambling move to Vegas, but when they find themselves ensconced in the gambling culture, they develop an addiction—and lose everything.
- ♣ The same thing happens to people who visit "Lost Wages"—only faster.
- ♣ Suicidal folks come to Vegas for one "last hurrah" before they check out, permanently.
- ♣ To make matters worse, the Great Recession has hit particularly hard in Las Vegas, and many residents have lost everything— without even gambling it away.

As it turns out, just living in Vegas is a gamble . . . to the death.

> THE VAST MAJORITY OF THOSE THAT CAME TO LAS VEGAS DID NOT COME HERE AND LOSE THEIR MONEY AND THEN COMMIT SUICIDE. THEY CAME HERE WITH THE IDEA OF MAKING THEIR LAST KIND OF 'HOORAY,' AND THEN THEY TOOK THEIR LIVES. AND THEY DID IT SO THAT THEY WOULDN'T BE DOING THAT AT HOME WHERE THEIR FAMILY MEMBERS WOULD FIND THEM.
>
> —Mike Murphy, county coroner

177. SAVE YOUR LIFE—LEAVE LAS VEGAS!

Las Vegas residents who move elsewhere lower their risk of suicide by 40 percent, according to *Psychiatric News*. Reason enough to skip town.

178. THE TOWER OF DEATH

There are certain places on our planet that draw the suicidal like flies to honey: the Golden Gate Bridge in San Francisco, the Empire State Building in New York City, Mount Mihara in Japan . . . and your average hotel room in Las Vegas. That's where most people pull the plug on their lives here in Sin City.

They hang themselves with sheets, like twenty-nine-year-old Hollywood actor David Strickland of *Suddenly Susan* fame did in his room at the Oasis Motel in 1999. Or they put a gun to their heads and pull the trigger, like sixty-four-year-old California businessman Lawrence Orbe did in a swank suite at the Four Seasons in 2004, despondent over the recent separation from his wife and money worries. Or they go off-strip, buy a 12-gauge shotgun from K-Mart, stick it in their mouths, and blow their brains out, like twenty-four-year-old University of Michigan student Elton Beamish did after he gambled away his financial aid money.

> **" I CAME HERE TO DRINK MYSELF TO DEATH. "**
> —Nicolas Cage as Ben Sanderson in *Leaving Las Vegas*

But perhaps the most dramatic suicide victims are the jumpers. The most popular spot to take a leap into that dark night is the Stratosphere Tower, which at 1,149 feet is the tallest building west of the Mississippi. But people have also thrown themselves off various parking garage roofs, from New York New York to the Aladdin. And the balconies that face the thirty-floor atrium inside the pyramid-shaped Luxor are also favored among suicidal jumpers.

179. THE UFC: A VEGAS INSTITUTION

The Ultimate Fighting Championship (UFC) events are kind of like those old wrestling shows your grandpa liked to watch, filled with blood and spectacle. There's one difference. The wrestling was faked. The UFC fights aren't.

That may be why this Las Vegas–based mixed martial arts promotion company (UFC) has become so successful. It has even managed to piss off Senator John McCain!

UFC 1 debuted in 1993 with the tagline, "There are no rules." You couldn't gouge out somebody's eye, but everything else, pretty much, was on the table: groin kicks, hair pulling, etc. Basically, UFC gave folks the chance to watch really big guys kick and punch the living shit out of each other. Awesome!

The fierceness of the events drew the ire of Senator McCain, who wanted to ban what he called "human cockfighting." The controversy led UFC to add some rules and gain at least a slight sheen of respectability . . . while still giving folks the chance to watch really big guys kick and punch the living shit out of each other. Still awesome!

MORE PROFITABLE THAN A CASINO

The UFC's parent company is owned by Lorenzo Fertitta, co-owner of the Station Casinos, which—as of this writing—remain in Chapter 11 (see #6). Fertitta resigned from Station Casinos in 2008 to focus on UFC.

CHAPTER 17

GANGS

180. CAPTAIN KIRK TAKES ON VEGAS GANGS

Some 13,000 people belong to gangs in Sin City—and another 2,500 consort with gang members. The gang unit at the Las Vegas Metropolitan Police Department is known as the Gang Crimes Bureau. Overseen by Captain Kirk Primas, the unit handles all criminal activity involving more than 500 gangs in Las Vegas—a myriad mix of crime that runs the gamut from graffiti and drug dealing to home invasions, robberies, gun trafficking, drive-by shootings, and hate crimes.

Surprisingly enough, it is the least of these crimes—graffiti—that often leads to violence. Rival gangs fight over graffiti territory—and painting over one gang's scribbling with one's own is all it takes to invite deadly retribution.

181. GANGS A-TWITTER

One of the most effective means of tracking gang activity in the city is through social networking—namely Facebook, MySpace, and Twitter. Like most young people, gang members often post their whereabouts and goings on online—and local law enforcement is there, watching and waiting.

> GANG MEMBERS ARE HOMEGROWN TERRORISTS.
>
> —Metro Gang Bureau Detective William Giblin

182. THE MOTORCYCLE WARS

If you think gang brawls are all about the color of your skin—think again. They're about the color of your clothes. In 2009, at Mr. D's Sportsbar & Grill in Las Vegas, two Flaming Knights Motorcycle gang members roared up sporting red and gold attire, inciting the ire of the Banditos Outlaw Motorcycle Gang and their compadres in the Dirty Outlaws Motorcycle Gang, who apparently believed that they owned the colors red and gold.

> " IT'S OKAY TO SHOW ALL YOUR COLORS. "
>
> —Luis Guzman

A confrontation ensued, and quickly escalated into a frenzy of stabbing with knives, box cutters, and flashlights, all in the attempt to purge the upstarts of their red and gold colors. The Flaming Knights were hurt in the motorcyclists' melee, one suffering stab wounds to his torso and the other suffering a broken ankle and a busted lip.

Twelve suspects have been arrested, charged, and were scheduled to go to trial in 2010.

All this over red and gold—when everyone knows there are 120 colors in the Crayola box of crayons.

183. THE MARRIAGE OF TRUE MINDS

What happens at a wedding chapel is a matter of public record—and we're not just talking marriages. At A Special Memory Wedding Chapel, adventurous couples can choose to be married in the drive-thru, or by Elvis, or even at the edge of the Grand Canyon. But on one fine day in 2008, the nuptials of two adventurous couples took a bad turn, when rival gang members arrived to attend their respective ceremonies.

The Hell's Angels bikers from one wedding met up with the Mongols' bikers from another wedding—and the honeymoon was over. Six people were injured as fists, feet, bottles, and trashcans flew. In 2010, thirteen people—eleven of whom were Hell's Angels—were indicted on felony charges of battery, assault, and attempted murder in connection with the incident.

> **MARRIAGE IS AN ADVENTURE, LIKE GOING TO WAR.**
>
> —Gilbert K. Chesterton

Part Six
PRIDE

LUXURIES AND INDULGENCES

184. SAYONARA SUCKERS

Want to be pampered Vegas-style? The Spa at ARIA has a whopping 80,000-square-foot Japanese-themed spa that offers sixty-two treatment rooms, as well three private spa suites that can accommodate up to eight people. You can customize your experience to include spa and salon services, dining, flower arrangements, and gift baskets. Spa packages range from three to twelve hours. A few special features you'll find at The Spa:

- ♣ A tranquil stone and water garden adorned with sacred Japanese Aji stones, blessed in Japan to inspire calmness and tranquility.
- ♣ A salt meditation room, Shio, features a wall of illuminated salt bricks, salt lamps, and lounge chairs that vibrate to music. The salt encourages healing of skin irritations and upper respiratory problems.
- ♣ A Japanese stone sauna, Ganbanyoku, has beds of heated black mineral stone that emit negative ions and infrared rays to relax muscles, improve blood circulation, increase metabolism, and eliminate toxins from the body. It has a "fire lounge" where you can relax before or after treatments.
- ♣ A Japanese-style open-air hot bath called Rotenburo.
- ♣ A 16,000-square-foot fitness center that offers personal training for private or group sessions, and may be tailored to fit personal needs.

The catch, aside from the prices, is that the spa is exclusively available to guests of City Center's hotels, which is par for the course in Vegas hotel spas.

185. SCRATCH N' SNIFF

The Spa at Mandarin Oriental Las Vegas offers 110-minute Signature Spa Therapies, using principles of Traditional Chinese Medicine and aroma-therapy designed to cure what ails you. You simply fill out a diagnostic questionnaire, designed to discover hidden aspects of your personality, and they evaluate the answers to select the perfect massage oil. Before a masseur slathers your skin with your oil, he or she will ask you to take a whiff to see if it's just right. Other treats available at The Spa Mandarin Oriental include:

- ♣ Chinese Foot Spa
- ♣ "Experience Showers" that use sound, light, and even smell to simulate an artic mist, an island storm, or a tropical rain.
- ♣ Turkish-style Hammam under a ceiling of luminous stars
- ♣ Laconium, a gently warming sauna
- ♣ Vitality Pool with panoramic views of Las Vegas Boulevard
- ♣ Ladies' Rhassoul bath

WHAT EXACTLY IS RHASSOUL?

Rhassoul is a rare and unprocessed Moroccan smectite clay rich in natural minerals. All clays draw out oils, toxins, impurities, as well as excess body and hormonal wastes, but smectite clay is the only one that deposits a rich cache of minerals that your body may or may not be able to produce. Rich in silica, magnesium, iron, calcium, potassium, and sodium, rhassoul is purported to help to maintain and preserve youthfulness, balance the oil level of the skin, control breakouts at any age, refine skin texture, and restore a glow to dull, dry skin.

186. NOTHING TRUMPS DIAMONDS

Of course The Spa at Trump offers signature gemstone treatments, using herbal oils that contain traces of diamonds, emeralds, rubies, or sapphires. Not only is it luxurious, they claim that each crystal plays a part in calming, healing, balancing, revitalizing, or purifying your body. The Spa also offers a black pearl rejuvenation facial that uses crushed black pearls and mineral-rich oyster shell extracts to tone your skin and improve tissue oxygenation, resulting in soft, supple, and luminous skin. Sounds positively decadent, doesn't it?

TRUMP THIS!

The waxing of the spa industry in the last decade has been nothing short of phenomenal. It is estimated that there are 12,000 spas throughout the United States, including day spas of which there are more than 8,700 and $5.4 billion in revenue. Resort hotel spas are the next largest category, with more than 1,600 spas bringing in $4.5 billion in revenue. Between 1999 and 2004, the industry experienced a 290 percent increase in resort hotel spas.

> THE FINAL KEY TO THE WAY I PROMOTE IS BRAVADO. I PLAY TO PEOPLE'S FANTASIES.
>
> —Donald Trump

187. UNDER THE YUM YUM TREE

If you can't afford diamonds, some Las Vegas spas use food to maximize pampering. Here are a few luxurious ones to sample next time you're in town—and hungry:

♣ The Spa at The Monte Carlo offers a champagne and caviar facial, which combines an enzyme peel and caviar/champagne cleansing mixture to reduce fine lines.

♣ The Nurture Spa and Salon offers an anti-aging chocolate and champagne facial that includes vitamin C and vanilla healing water, leaving your skin ultra-hydrated.

♣ The bathhouse spa at THEhotel at Mandalay Bay offers a Yummy Mocha Java Sculpting Treatment. You begin with a chocolate or cappuccino sugar scrub, followed an organic mocha java masque (enhanced with green teas, marine algae, and aloe vera), designed to increase firmness in your skin, and finish with a slathering of cappuccino cream, designed to leave your skin soft and silky. They also offer a crème brûlée body treatment, including crème brûlée mani-pedi.

♣ The Spa at Green Valley Ranch Resort & Spa offers the Green Tea Wrap. First, your skin is scrubbed with grape seeds from California's Napa Valley, then wrapped with cloths steeped in green tea, seaweed, and ginger root, designed to boost your body's metabolism. The treatment ends with a massage, which includes a special blend of exotic essential oils and protein cream.

" MY THERAPIST TOLD ME THE WAY TO ACHIEVE TRUE INNER PEACE IS TO FINISH WHAT I START. SO FAR TODAY, I HAVE FINISHED TWO BAGS OF M&MS AND A CHOCOLATE CAKE. I FEEL BETTER ALREADY. "
—Dave Barry

188. SPANK ME BABY

The Oleksandra Spa & Salon offers a wet n' wild fifteen-minute Russian Banya sauna. First, you lie down on the bench and relax as your spa therapist pours water and essential oil over hot rocks. As you heat up, your therapist uses a warmed oak leaf whisk to wave heat over your body. Once you're relaxed and cozy, he or she then uses the whisk to stroke, brush, and tap your body. It's designed to increase circulation, relax muscle tissue, remove dead skin cells, and flush toxins out of your body. After your "gentle spanking," you're invited to enjoy a cool, refreshing rain shower.

DAS BOOTS

If you long for boots to stomp all over you, you might want to sign up for an ashiatsu at the Palazzo. What is it, you ask? It's a deep compression massage in which the therapist holds onto overhead bars as he or she walks up and down and across your body. They say this invigorating massage stimulates your body's lymphatic system. Okay, then, start stomping . . .

> WHEN I WANT TO REWARD MYSELF I GET A RELAXING MASSAGE.
> —Eva Longoria

189. WHO'S YOUR DADDY?

Just kidding about the daddy part, but if you're curious to know what secrets may lie in your DNA, you can gamble, relax at a spa, and map your DNA at the same resort. The Grand Spa at The MGM offers "SpaGen," a revolutionary DNA process that tests an individual's overall well being. All you do is fill out an in-depth health, diet, and lifestyle questionnaire, and then spa technicians swab the inside of your cheek. The DNA sample is then forwarded to a lab for analysis. About two weeks later, you'll receive an extensive summary describing your nutritional deficiencies, as well tips for achieving beauty and overall wellness. If you like, you can also order a once-a-month personalized package of nutritional supplements designed just for you.

> NO ONE I KNOW OF HAS EVER HAD THIS EXPERIENCE—WHERE YOU HAD TO SIT AND WAIT AND WAIT FOR A DNA TEST TO COME BACK JUST SO YOU CAN WRITE THE LAST PAGE OF THE BOOK.
>
> —Joseph Wambaugh, author

190. SCENTSATIONAL

If you love a unique scent and have a nose for roses, The Spa at The Four Seasons offers guests an opportunity to create their own signature Ajne Rare and Precious Perfumes fragrance. Spa patrons meet individually with a mélanger—a spa specialist trained to create a customized fragrance— who helps you select your favorite scent and then infuses the fragrance into one of Ajne's handmade Bohemian flacons, combining your selected fragrance with all-nature oils designed to balance body and mind. The blend can also be added to spa products for a customized spa treatment or to spa products you can purchase to take home. Ajne's founder, Jane Hendler, has created custom fragrances for celebrities such as Reese Witherspoon, Hilary Swank, Kanye West, America Ferrera, Jessica Biel, Pierce Brosnan, Kate Walsh, Patrick Dempsey, and Debra Messing, among others.

> A MAN HAS HIS DISTINCTIVE PERSONAL SCENT WHICH HIS WIFE, HIS CHILDREN, AND HIS DOG CAN RECOGNIZE. A CROWD HAS A GENERALIZED STINK.
>
> —W.H. Auden

BEE STILL MY HEART

If you're a bee lover, you may well adore the Canyon Ranch Spa Club at the Venetian, where you can relax in its Middle East-inspired Rasul chamber in the shape of a beehive. Once you and your beloved are coated in therapeutic muds, you enter the beehive chamber for an extensive herbal steam treatment, replete with a faux starlit sky above. After you're thoroughly relaxed — and cooked — your treatment ends with a refreshingly delightful rain shower.

191. BRING ON THE OIL

One thing you've figured out by now is that a multitude of enticing spa options await you in Vegas. Below are some of the more unusual choices.

- ♣ At the Mandalay Bay Moorea Beach area, you can cool down by indulging in ten-minute Mai Tai, Pina Colada, or Margarita scented moisturizing *body* shots. And if you're feeling a little pale, you can order your body shots with a tan accelerator.
- ♣ The Spa Bellagio offers a Watsu massage, an aquatic massage combining Zen Shiatsu and the element of floating in warm water.
- ♣ The Reliquary Spa at The Hard Rock Hotel Tower attracts naughty girls who enjoy wrapping themselves around a stripper pole in its dancing studio.
- ♣ The Royal Treatment Spa at Excalibur has a tanning bed that features a flat-screen TV built into the top, so you can watch TV while tanning.
- ♣ At the Imperial Palace Spa you can sample a massage with the optional biofreeze cryotherapy if you will for deep relief of aching muscles, joint pain, and backaches.
- ♣ At The Spa at Wynn you can sample their signature spa treatment, an eighty-minute Good Luck Ritual that equates to feng shui for

the body, designed to boost your chances to achieve wealth, health, prosperity, happiness, and harmony.

> ### MUTUAL MASSAGE
> At the Grand Vacation Spa at the Hilton, guests can opt for the Champagne Couple's Retreat, in which a massage therapist comes up to the room and teaches the couple how to give a professional massage to each other.

> " MY EARS TURN ME ON LIKE NOTHING ELSE, THEY MUST BE MY MOST EROGENOUS ZONE. JUST HAVING MY EARS KNEADED IS LIKE A FULL-BODY MASSAGE. "
>
> —Rebecca Romjin

192. FOLLOW YOUR NOSE

Well aware that scents can stimulate memories and evoke emotions, nearly every Las Vegas resort has a metal device the size of a breadbox attached to their ventilation systems that they use to vaporize expensive, highly aromatic oils into the ducts. The Mirage hired Mark Peltier, president of AromaSys, to install the first system in 1991. Since then, the use of smell has spread up and down the Strip. Peltier, who markets systems throughout the world, strives to make the hotels smell like the ideal version of their location—in South Florida he uses citrus scents and at a Colorado ski resort he'll use woodsy scents. But in Las Vegas, each resort supplied by AromaSys has a signature theme. The Mirage chose a Polynesian scent, Mandalay Bay a Southeast Asian scent, and the Bellagio the scent of Northern Italy. The most provocative smell belongs to the Venetian, a "seduction" scent that vaporizes heavy doses of musk to bathe guests in a scent that is "strong, soothing, and sensuous." According to Peltier, who prefers a lighter scent, the Venetian guests must find it very appealing as the resort sells a lot of their signature scent as room sprays and candles.

SMELLS 101

Behind every pleasing scent there's a pleasant association. In general, certain commonly used scents are chosen for their pleasant associations:

- ♠ Citrus smells are refreshing.
- ♠ Floral smells are relaxing.
- ♠ Herbaceous smells like peppermint are usually relaxing but can also be invigorating.
- ♠ Cedar and other wood smells are relaxing and soothing.

" THE [SIGNATURE SCENTS OF THE] WYNN AND ENCORE RESORTS ARE VERY UNUSUAL, YOU MAY NEVER SMELL ANYTHING LIKE THAT IN THE WORLD. MR. WYNN HAS EXTRAORDINARY SENSORY IDEAS AND KNOWS WHAT HE WANTS. IT'S MORE OF A CO-CREATIVE PROCESS WITH HIM. "

—Mark Peltier, president of AromaSys

193. FREE BOOB JOBS FOR EVERYONE!

What happens in Vegas, stays in Vegas—except for the great ideas that are conceived here and then taken home for fun and profit. Here anything goes—and for some people, that giddy freedom inspires genius.

The popular website *Myfreeimplants.com* is the perfect example. Picture this: Rowdy guys at a bachelor party in Vegas hanging out with some beautiful girls. One of the gentlemen compliments the girl with the biggest rack. She confesses that she just had her girls done, and her flat friend bemoans the fact that she can't raise the $6,000 to buy herself a pair. The guys—charitable to a man—pass the hat for her new boob job. Next thing you know, they've started a website and are raising money for poor disadvantaged small-breasted women everywhere.

Now that's what we call a Vegas brainstorm.

> **SEE, THAT'S WHAT'S GREAT ABOUT AMERICA! HERE ARE MEN LEND-ING A HELPING HAND TO COMPLETE STRANGERS. SEE, THAT'S WHAT MAKES OUR COUNTRY GREAT!**
>
> —Jay Leno discussing Myfreeimplants.com

CHAPTER 19

BIGGER, STRONGER, FASTER

194. THE LEGACY OF HOWARD HUGHES

What do you do when you've got $546 million burning a hole in your pocket? Well, if you're Howard Hughes, you buy up most of the Las Vegas Strip's major properties, pushing out the mob and making the city a stronghold for legitimate corporations.

Before he became a germophobic weirdo, Hughes would gamble in various Vegas spots, luscious showgirls on his arm. By 1966, however, Hughes was into his "bashful billionaire" phase.

> HOW MANY MORE OF THESE TOYS ARE AVAILABLE? LET'S BUY 'EM ALL!
> —Howard Hughes

Pockets filled with cash from the sale of his TWA airline stock, Hughes checked into the Desert Inn. He had an entire floor to himself. After ten days, New Year's Eve rapidly approaching, representatives of the mob-owned property wanted Hughes out. Rather than budge, Hughes bought the Desert Inn. He didn't stop there. Hughes bought up the Sands, the Castaways, the Silver Slipper, and the Frontier.

Then it was all over. Hughes left for the Bahamas and never returned to Sin City. But his legacy remains. The mob is gone, but *Fortune* 500 companies are all over the city.

195. THAT'S BOULDER DAM, TOURIST!

Yeah, that's right. Boulder Dam. *Not* Hoover Dam. Only out-of-towners call this concrete structure that bridges Nevada and Arizona the Hoover Dam. Locals know its correct name.

But these smug locals are equally stupid. The dam was *not* built in Boulder Canyon; it was built in Black Canyon. Why did the name "Boulder Dam" take off anyway? That's easy. Most people, whether in Arizona, Nevada, or Appleton, are geographically challenged. That's why.

DAM, IT'S BIG
The largest dam in the United States is the Oroville Dam in Butte County, California. It stands 770 feet tall. Boulder Dam is only 726 feet tall.

Boulder Dam is an impressive structure, but it's not one of the world's largest dams by volume or by height. It's not even the largest dam in the United States. But so what? It's the closest dam to Las Vegas, and that makes it the coolest "goddamn dam" in the world.

The dam's construction began during the administration of President Herbert Hoover, and one of his lackeys decided to name the dam in honor of his boss, even though most people associated the former engineer with Hoovervilles, cardboard box towns that grew up across the country in the wake of the Great Depression.

No wonder locals don't want to name their dam after a guy who lost America millions. It might be bad luck, and you know how superstitious gamblers are.

196. PINBALL HALL OF FAME

Kids weaned on DSes, XBoxes, and Wiis wouldn't know a pinball machine if it walked up and bit them on their childhood-obesity-challenged behinds. They've never experienced the joys of putting "body English" into a game, flirting constantly with the danger of tilting a machine and ending their game prematurely.

Fortunately, Las Vegas has just the place for kids and their aging parents and grandparents who remember a time when video games were just science fiction. The Pinball Hall of Fame opened on Tropicana Avenue in 2006.

> " IN THE EARLY 1980S, YOU COULD HAVE A PILE OF DOG CRAP HOOKED UP TO A VIDEO MONITOR, AND PEOPLE WOULD PUT A QUARTER IN IT FOR PLAY. "
>
> —Tim Arnold

The brainchild of arcade owner and pinball aficionado Tim Arnold, the Pinball Hall of Fame features some 400 games that have been lovingly restored by Arnold since he first moved his collection from Lansing to Sin City in 1990.

Proceeds from the Pinball Hall of Fame go to the Salvation Army, which makes these machines among the very few coin-eating monsters in Vegas that actually help people, rather than transforming them into selfish, greedy, gambling addicts. Not that there's anything *wrong* with selfish, greedy, gambling addicts.

197. WHEN THE LIGHTS GO OUT IN LAS VEGAS

Even the junkyards in Las Vegas are cool. For proof, drive along Encanto Drive, just west of the Strip, and look through the fence that surrounds the Young Electric Sign Company's (YESCO's) neon graveyard.

Salt Lake City–based YESCO is responsible for some of the most famous neon signs ever to shine down on debauched gambling alcoholics.

Vegas Vic, the cowboy who dominates Fremont Street in Glitter Gulch, is a YESCO product. So is the so-called moving eraser that graces Wynn Las Vegas.

Signs that have outgrown their usefulness wind up in the neon graveyard. A silver slipper from the eponymous and long-defunct Silver Slipper sits next to one of the original Aladdin's magic lamps. All of the old Binion's Horseshoe signs are scattered amid various wedding chapel marquees.

The graveyard often graces photo shoots, but it's open to the public only through the occasional guided tour. YESCO is in the process of creating a site at which many of these old signs will be available for viewing, and some of the company's works can be seen at the Neon Museum (see #198).

198. BRIGHT LIGHTS, SIN CITY

Neon is to Las Vegas what iambic pentameter was to Shakespeare: a medium that brings artistry to vivid life. By day, Sin City isn't very impressive. By night, it's paradise, a wonderland, a garden of Earthly delights.

SEEING NEON

For information regarding Neon Museum tours at YESCO, log on to *www.neonmuseum.org/tours.html* or e-mail *tours@neonmuseum.org*.

In 1996, the city unveiled the first portion of its Neon Museum along Fremont Street in downtown Las Vegas. Ten signs from the golden age of Vegas are on display, including the Hacienda's horse and rider, Aladdin's lamp, and The Red Barn, a long-gone watering hole.

Plans are underway to expand the museum to include the famous "neon graveyard" in Young Electric Sign Company's (YESCO's) storage lot (see #197).

In 2006, the visually stunning lobby of the La Concha Motel was saved from the wrecking ball and moved to YESCO's property. Soon, it will be a visitor's center and gateway to the neon boneyard.

Maybe then, finally, folks will stop trying to sneak into the neon graveyard, which, for a time, YESCO actually claimed did not exist.

199. THE RHINESTONE PIANO PLAYER LIVES ON

No one sported chiffon, fur, and rhinestones—while claiming to be heterosexual—with more panache than Wladziu Valentino Liberace. He already was a television star and international concert draw before he arrived on the Strip.

> THANK YOU FOR YOUR VERY AMUSING REVIEW. AFTER READING IT, IN FACT, MY BROTHER GEORGE AND I CRIED ALL THE WAY TO THE BANK.
>
> —Liberace

Liberace opened the Riviera Hotel and Casino in 1955, and his $50,000-per-week salary was, at the time, the highest amount ever paid to a Las Vegas performer. Maybe that's why Liberace maintained a home in Sin City.

He also opened a Las Vegas museum dedicated to, what else, himself. The museum, which opened in 1979, houses dozens of the showman's costumes, pianos, cars, and other ephemera, all of which gives visitors perfect visual representations of the word "gaudy."

The Liberace Museum remains one of the Vegas's most popular tourist attractions, and it is known not only for its eye-popping artifacts but also for the frighteningly butch women who work the gift shop and admission desk.

200. RACE TO THE BANK

Think NASCAR is just for Southerners, you're wrong. Since the Las Vegas Speedway opened in 1996, it has attracted huge crowds.

The $200 million complex seats 150,000 honorary rednecks several times a year. Races include the Sam's Town 300, sponsored by one of Vegas's oldest locals' only casinos; the Qwik Liner Las Vegas 350; and the *piece de resistance,* the Shelby American, a Cup Series race in late February/ early March.

> **THE MINT 400**
>
> The (dirty old) granddaddy of Las Vegas auto racing is the Mint 400, called The Great American Desert Race. It was sponsored by the now-defunct Mint Casino from 1968 to 1988. In 2010, its founder, Norm Johnson, announced plans to resurrect the Mint 400.

The speedway has four tracks. Two are ovals, one is a drag strip, and the main track, which is 1.5 miles long. That makes the Las Vegas Speedway just that, a speedway, not a "superspeedway," which is a track at least two miles long.

So, if you're in Vegas at the right time—and you're interested in some form of incest—then you should check out Sin City's NASCAR track.

201. THE ROCK 'N' ROLL MARATHON

For most people who come to Sin City, "exercise" involves pulling slot handles and retching into toilets. But Las Vegas is also home to a marathon that just began its fifth decade.

The first Las Vegas Marathon was run in 1967. Since then, the event has changed hands a few times. In 2009, Competitor Group added Sin

City to its "Rock 'n' Roll" marathon series, which offers live bands and cheer squads at each mile of the course. A headliner gives a concert for competitors after the race is over. Kenyans Christopher Toroitich and Caroline Rotich were the 2009 winners.

In the early days, the marathon stayed away from the Strip, but since 2005, the Las Vegas Marathon has marked one of the rare occasions when one of the most famous streets in the world is entirely closed to vehicular traffic.

202. RIDING HIGH

The Stratosphere, at the far end of the famous Las Vegas Strip, has one thing going for it: thrill rides.

> ### NO MORE HIGH ROLLER
> One of the first Stratosphere rides was the High Roller, a roller coaster that went around the top of the tower. It was slow and often broke down, so it was discontinued in 2005. What's left are some, admittedly, spectacular thrills.

All of the rides atop the 1,149-foot tower make use of the fact that the structure is the tallest tower in the United States. The Big Shot zooms folks up to the top of the spire and back down at about forty-five miles per hour. The X-Scream is a giant seesaw that dangles riders a thousand feet above the crack whores that populate this end of the Strip. Insanity, the newest Stratosphere ride, looks like a claw extending from the lip of the tower. Riders get in the cars, which are spun around at high speeds, causing a tilt that leaves riders parallel to the ground. Finally, Skyjump is like a bungee jump on steroids. One jumps from the tower, attached to a guide wire, and falls 855 feet—or 108 stories—to the Strip below. Watch out for those crack whores, buddy!

203. WILD RIDE THROUGH THE BIG APPLE

The days when casinos gave away the entertainment in order to attract gamblers are *gone*. Case in point: New York New York's roller coaster, once called the Manhattan Express.

> ### PRETTY MUCH THE SAME AND FREE
> You can get a *3D New York Roller Coast Rush* app for your iPhone, free. Here's the link: www.digitalchocolate.com/iphone/.

Unless an orgasm comes at the end of it, no thrill ride is worth fourteen dollars a pop. But this is Vegas, baby! You're paying for the steak, the sizzle, and even the glass of ice water.

The tallest hill on The Roller Coaster (original name, that) is 203 feet, and the top speed is 67 miles per hour. Not bad . . . but not much. The best thing about the attraction is that it moves you through the simulated Manhattan skyline. Hey, I'm taller than the Chrysler Building! I'm like King Kong on the Empire State Building! That sort of thing.

204. TAKE THE PLUNGE: SAY I DO

The Roller Coaster at New York New York (see #203) also offers regular packages for the ultimate plunge: marriage. For $600 to $700, you and your wedding party can have a service on board a thrill ride. Maybe you'll even get lucky, and your mother-in-law-to-be will have a heart attack and die from the thrill!

205. YIPPEE KI YAY, LAS VEGAS!

Hoity toity in Sin City isn't relegated merely to the high-roller portions of the Strip's crown jewel properties. You also can find it—and a taste of the pastoral life—at Clark County's Horseman's Park.

The park includes a 53,000-square-foot rodeo arena that can hold 1,300 people. Such events as the annual Las Vegas High School Rodeo are held there. The Flamingo Arena is slightly smaller and holds four hundred. The Horseman's Park also includes a 13,500-square-foot cutting area. ("Cutting" is an equestrian event that involves separating a calf from a pack and roping it.)

> "BEST RATE IN TOWN, IF YOU'RE A HORSE!"
> —Clark County Parks and Recreation website

The Horseman's Park also offers stabling for folks who travel with their horses. Or, stables can be rented for locals who are going out of town. For a city focused on attaining as much coin as possible, stable rates are pretty cheap: ten bucks a night.

The public can use the park's arenas when events are not being held since everyone who's anyone owns a horse. This *is* the West, after all.

206. THE BEST DEAL IN VEGAS: ADVENTUREDOME

The granddaddy of all Las Vegas thrill rides is the Adventuredome— formerly Grand Slam Canyon—at Circus Circus. For just ten bucks more than the cost of a *single* ride on a *single* roller coaster at New York New

York (see #201), you can enjoy twenty-five rides and attractions all under a sparkling pink dome.

NOT JUST FOR KIDS
Contrary to popular belief, when Circus Circus opened in 1968 it was *not* targeted primarily to kids. It was filled with peep shows and other forms of adult entertainment. Creator Jay Sarno was just a guy who liked circuses.

Launched in 1993, right at the time Las Vegas was (temporarily) trying to transform itself into a family-friendly vacation locale, the Circus Circus theme park is 350,000 square feet. Some of the rides are for kids, and some are for adults like Chaos, which spins you around and upside down; the double-loop Canyon Blaster roller coaster; and the Rim Runner. No, that last one isn't X-rated. It's just a white water rafting type thing.

The Adventuredome is top-heavy with kiddie rides, but it's still a pretty good deal.

207. LAKE MEAD: OASIS IN THE DESERT

Though not known for water, the Las Vegas area is home to the country's largest reservoir, Lake Mead (see #133).

The lake is formed by the Hoover Dam and covers about 247 square miles. Lake Mead holds some nine trillion gallons of water, or at least it's supposed to. The desert, already dry to begin with, has been in a drought for most of the last ten years. Between 2000 and 2008, the water level dropped from 1,215 to just over 1,000 feet deep, leaving stark white "bathtub rings" on display.

Hmm. Folks in expensive gated communities have lush, green lawns. Fountains are everywhere on the Strip. Hello, Bellagio? Lake Mead called. You're taking all the water. Desert? What desert?

As long as Lake Mead holds up, however, it provides visitors plenty of recreational opportunities. The lake has five marinas, offers great fishing, and has any number of coves for exploring and swimming. About the only thing you won't find on the water is casinos.

THE NAME'S THE THING

Lake Mead is named for Elwood Mead, commissioner of the U.S. Bureau of Reclamation from 1924 to 1936, while the Boulder (now called Hoover) Dam was being planned.

208. CALLING ALL MOUNTAIN LOVERS

If you don't even realize Mt. Charleston exists, then you're forgiven. After all, who needs rugged scenic beauty when you're surrounded by topless hotties and blackjack tables?

MORE MOUNT CHARLESTON FACTS

Mt. Charleston's peak is 11,916 feet above sea level. It's the eighth-highest peak in Nevada. Mt. Charleston is part of the Spring Mountains National Recreation Area. Mt. Charleston is one of the few places near Las Vegas that's not likely to have VD-encrusted toilet seats.

Mt. Charleston is that mountain you can see from the Strip that, roughly half the year, has snow at its peak. It's only thirty-five miles from Vegas, so it's well worth a visit.

In the winter, you'll find a small ski resort up there (see #171). At other times of the year, you'll find numerous hiking trails, 200 campsites, and 150 picnic tables. You could even opt to stay in a lodge on the mountain, instead of down in the valley of sin.

Mt. Charleston is a great place to go to clear one's head. Las Vegas is nonstop hyper-reality, and, while exciting and fun, it can be draining. A quick trip up to Mount Charleston can be the cure for the partied-out blues.

209. MOVIES SHOT IN VEGAS

Diamonds are Forever, the 1971 Bond flick that replaced action with camp, was among the first films not only to feature Las Vegas as a location but actually to be *shot* in Sin City. The plot? Who cares? Basically, at one point, Bond, James Bond, stays in a hotel owned by a Howard Hughes character. Mayhem and zaniness ensues.

Las Vegas was represented in the 1980s by the fourth Cheech and Chong movie, *Things Are Tough All Over*, which moved back and forth between Vegas and Chicago. The film featured the loveable stoners and a crop of very non-pc Arabs. What's the movie about? Dope smoking in Vegas!

> I'LL TAKE THE FULL ODDS ON THE TEN, TWO HUNDRED ON THE HARD WAY, THE LIMIT ON ALL THE NUMBERS, TWO HUNDRED AND FIFTY ON THE ELEVEN. THANK YOU VERY MUCH.
>
> —James Bond

By the 1990s, all kinds of films were being set in, or at least featured numerous scenes set in, Sin City. *Mars Attacks!*, a Tim Burton film, featured the real-life implosion of the Landmark Hotel and Casino. *Rush Hour 2*, from 2001, contained scenes shot in the Desert Inn, just before it was imploded. And, just to keep the stoner vibe alive, a Las Vegas road trip was featured in 2007's *Knocked Up*, starring Seth Rogen.

210. RAINBOW SIX: VEGAS

An international counter-terrorism unit foils a plot to blow up a huge dam sitting just outside of a large, gambling-filled city. That's the gist of the video game, "Tom Clancy's Rainbow Six: Vegas."

The 2006 game (a newer edition was released in 2010) was the fifth in the wildly popular gaming series, and it makes extensive use of Sin City locales, altering them slightly to avoid paying greedy casino corporations even more money. For example, a kidnapped weapons researcher is rescued from the Vertigo Spire, which is clearly based on the Stratosphere, except that the Spire actually seems like a cool place, while the Stratosphere is kinda lame and somewhat seedy.

> I JUST WISH THE GAME WAS A LITTLE LONGER OR EVEN A LITTLE
> HARDER. I RECOMMEND THIS GAME TO ANYONE!
>
> —Juan Deanda, review of "Rainbow Six: Vegas," from zergwatch.com

The Rainbow Six team arrives just in time at the Nevada (i.e., Hoover a.k.a Boulder) Dam, defuses the bomb, and kills the bad guy . . . or in this case, gal. Hooray! It's over, gamers! Now you can switch back to surfing Internet porn!

Part Seven
ENVY

CHAPTER 20

LARCENY

211. THERE'S A TOURIST SUCKER BORN EVERY MINUTE

Las Vegas is the tourist town of tourist towns—and where there are tourists, there's crime. Theft is the most common crime against tourists, but you can also be the victim of aggravated assault, sexual assault, even homicide.

Crime rates across the board—from property theft to murder—are higher here than the national average. Smart tourists take precautions, so when you visit Las Vegas, be smart and:

- ♣ Stick close to the Strip.
- ♣ Never walk from the Strip to Fremont St.
- ♣ Put your valuables in the hotel safe.
- ♣ Watch your pockets—and purses.
- ♣ Always keep your hands on your luggage.
- ♣ Lock the extra deadbolt on your hotel room.

> **AND THEN WE'RE GONNA FIND OUR BEST FRIEND DOUG, AND THEN WE'RE GONNA GIVE HIM A BEST FRIEND HUG. DOUG, DOUG, OH, DOUG, DOUGIE, DOUGIE, DOUG, DOUG! BUT IF HE'S BEEN MURDERED BY CRYSTAL METH TWEAKERS . . . WELL, THEN WE'RE SHIT OUT OF LUCK.**
> —Ed Helms as Stu Price in *The Hangover*

212. CRYSTAL = CRIME

A shocking 90 percent of the crime committed in the state of Nevada is related to methamphetamine, according to the Nevada Department of Health and Human Services (see #89 and #90).

Add in the meth connection, and that means when you get mugged or pick-pocketed or assaulted, it's most likely by a raging crystal meth addict. Nice.

> A SIXTEENTH OF AN OUNCE OF METH COSTS ABOUT $80 TO $100. BIG-TIME USERS CAN USE TWICE AS MUCH AS THAT IN A DAY. A LOT OF BURGLARIES AND ROBBERIES ARE THE DIRECT RESULT OF USERS WANTING TO BE ABLE TO PURCHASE THESE DRUGS.
>
> —Sgt. Erik Lloyd, Las Vegas Police Department

213. THE JUICEMAN ARRESTETH

Almost more than a decade after a murder acquittal with which just about everyone had a hard time agreeing, justice finally caught up with Orenthal James Simpson . . . at, of all places, a locals' casino in Las Vegas.

On September 13, 2007, a group of men broke into a room at the Palace Station and took—at gunpoint allegedly—a bunch of O.J. sports memorabilia owned by a man named Bruce Fromong. The ringleader was O.J. himself, who was later sentenced to thirty-three years in prison. In a final bit of poetic justice, Simpson received his sentence on October 3, 2008 . . . thirteen years to the day of his acquittal for murder.

> I'M O.J. SIMPSON. HOW AM I GOING TO THINK THAT I'M GOING TO ROB SOMEBODY AND GET AWAY WITH IT? BESIDES, I THOUGHT WHAT HAPPENS IN LAS VEGAS STAYS IN LAS VEGAS.
>
> —O.J. Simpson

214. GOD STRIKES BACK!

Clearly, God hates casinos . . . at least locals' only casinos.

In July of 1998, God smote heavily the Palace Station (see #6), causing fire to spread throughout the property's twenty-first floor. No one was killed, but four people were injured in the blaze.

Many believed the fire was a result of lightning, but we have a different theory. Folks have been calling Las Vegas the Sodom and Gomorrah of the Western Hemisphere at least since the 1940s. Of course, many of those same folks also have been frequent visitors to Sin City, but at least they feel guilty about it on Sunday morning.

> **I JUST WANT TO KNOW ABOUT MY NICKELS . . . THERE MUST HAVE BEEN AT LEAST 2,000 NICKELS IN THERE THAT ARE MINE.**
> —Marlene Runbert

So, God got busy righting wrongs. First, He struck the place with a thunderbolt. Then, He went about causing some folks, such as Marlene Runbert, to lose their ill-gotten gains. Right at the time she lined up three sevens on a nickel slot machine, she was forced to evacuate the casino and leave behind her spoils.

God wanted to attack one of Steve Wynn's places, but He could not because Wynn is apparently richer than God.

215. THE VEGAS CONNECTION: DUNBAR ARMORED CAR HEIST

Although it didn't occur in Las Vegas, the largest cash robbery in United States history had a Las Vegas connection: Thomas Lee Johnson. Johnson wasn't the mastermind of the Dunbar Armored Robbery, but he was a childhood friend of ringleader Allen Pace.

On September 12, 1997, Pace put his plan into action. A regional safety inspector for Dunbar Armored, he knew which bags of money held the greatest denominations. He had keys to the door. He knew how to avoid security cameras. And he knew that on Friday nights, the vault would be open because large amounts of money were to be moved to businesses for the weekend.

A GOOD YEAR FOR THIEVES

The three largest cash robberies in U.S. history (so far) all took place in 1997 and all were related to armored cars or armored car headquarters.

Pace and his five childhood friends, including Johnson, pulled off a perfect robbery and drove off in a U-Haul filled with $18.9 million. A piece of taillight from the U-Haul wound up cracking the case.

Pace received twenty-four years in prison. Johnson was arrested and charged with twenty-four counts of money laundering. He must have been good at his job, because $10 million remains unaccounted for.

216. MERRY CHRISTMAS, PALACE STATION

Thirty-six thousand dollars sounds like nothing compared to a million, but it *was* "free money."

On December 14, 2009, at least two men robbed an armored car driver at gunpoint in front of the Palace Station, a locals'-only place just off the Strip. This, by the way, is the same property that has endured lightning strikes (see #214), bankruptcy (see #6), and a gun-toting O.J. Simpson (see #213). Geez . . . why does the Palace Station get all of Sin City's bad karma?

At first, the amount of money reported stolen was a million bucks. Later, however, the casino stated that the thieves got away with $36,000 in cash.

Thirty-six thousand? It hardly seems worth it! That's less than a valet makes at one of the swanky spots on the Strip. Nonetheless, the two—reportedly—white, middle-aged dudes who took the money seem to have gotten away with the crime.

> IT WAS $36,000, NOT $1 MILLION. STILL, A LOT OF LOOT! SOMEONE IS GOING TO HAVE A MERRY CHRISTMAS, IF THE COPS DON'T FIND THEM.
> —"Ricky," from a blog posting responding to the story on ktnv.com

Maybe they took their loot and went to see one of Cirque du Soleil's shows. Thirty-six thousand would just about cover that.

217. THE LONG AND SHORT OF ARMORED CAR ROBBERY

Armored cars and their drivers do *not* have a good track record in Sin City. They've been involved in a number of thefts. One would think, then, that armored car companies would be even more vigilant and put a stop to these robberies. But this is America; we don't learn from the past.

On February 18, 2010, a Loomis armored truck guard was getting ready to make a cash drop at a Bank of America on East Charleston, a part of Las Vegas that is generally thought to be pretty safe. As he was carrying a money bag into the bank, two guys robbed him at gunpoint and took off in a Honda.

> THAT'S THE MOST IMPORTANT THING [THAT THE GUARD WASN'T SERIOUSLY INJURED], AND I HOPE THEY RECOVER THE MONEY.
> —John Ortiz, bank customer

The guard at the wheel, apparently, did not even realize anything was amiss. That's the sort of vigilance that leads to on-the-job safety!

The two thieves got away with $86,000. Described as being 5'6" or so, perhaps these particular short robbers were just overcoming an inherent Napoleon complex. You know, steal stuff, feel big.

218. THE BRAINWASHING OF HEATHER TALLCHIEF

A woman is "brainwashed" into committing crimes. Nope, this isn't about the Manson family or Patty Hearst. It's about one of the biggest heists ever to take place in Sin City.

After more than a decade on the run, Heather Tallchief turned herself in to authorities for her part in the 1993 Loomis Armored Car Heist, which resulted in over $3 million stolen from Circus Circus.

Tallchief, a driver for Armored Loomis, claimed to have worked with her boyfriend, Roberto Solis, to steal the money. Las Vegas native Tallchief drove off with the money while other Loomis "employees" filled ATM machines.

> **I TRULY FEEL THIS IS THE RIGHT THING TO DO.**
>
> —Heather Tallchief, after surrendering to authorities

In 2005, Tallchief surrendered, claiming she wanted her ten-year-old son to be able to live a normal life. She had spent the past ten years living and working in Amsterdam. For her crime, Tallchief was given sixty-three months in prison and ordered to pay back the $3 million.

The Web is filled with sites with a "free Heather Tallchief" theme because she claimed she did the crime only after Solis brainwashed her. Yep. Sure. Uh-huh. Solis remains at large.

CHAPTER 21

MAKING IT BIG

219. *DANKE SHOEN,* WAYNE NEWTON

He may be the textbook example of "cheesy lounge singer," but Sin City just wouldn't be Sin City without the Midnight Idol. Wayne Newton first performed in Las Vegas in 1958, when he was still in high school. More than fifty years later, he's played 30,000 shows in locations all over Sin City. Not bad for a guy whose voice is an acquired taste.

WAIT A MINUTE...THE *BEACH BOYS?*

Outside of Las Vegas, Wayne Newton is perhaps most famous for an incident that occurred in 1983. Then-Secretary of the Interior James "trees-cause-air-pollution" Watt disinvited the Beach Boys from a summer concert to take place on the Washington Mall because they were just too decadently rock 'n' roll for him. The group was replaced by Wayne.

What Newton lacks in pipes he more than makes up for in sheer, cheesy, over-the-top, *people-I-love-ya* charisma. He goes all out every night, sweaty manscaped chest exposed, arms gesticulating wildly. No wonder aging ladies still toss their granny panties in his direction! You feel like you can't write about the guy without ending every sentence with an exclamation point!

But Wayne is in on the joke. He knows he's cheesy and that some find his sweaty emoting unconscionable. Ah, eff 'em if they can't take a joke.

220. LAS VEGAS LITTLE THEATRE

Think Las Vegas entertainment is all tits, asses, and has-beens? Well, it is, pretty much. But there *is* another category of entertainers—never-will-be's. The place to find them is the Las Vegas Little Theatre (LVLT).

By Las Vegas standards, this community theater is positively ancient. It dates back to the Disco Era! Jack Bell and Jack Nickolson (that's *Nikolson*, not *Nicholson*, so don't get excited) started the theater in 1978, in an effort to provide locals with opportunities for legitimate theater . . . as though topless revues *weren't* legitimate theater.

WHY GO TO THE LVLT?

Tickets for Las Vegas Little Theatre productions run about $20 to $25. Tickets for Cirque du Soleil's Bellagio show, *O, start* at $102. You do the math.

In addition to showcasing such productions as *A Streetcar Named Desire* and *I Love You, You're Perfect, Now Change*, the LVLT also offers acting and theater production classes. It has both a main stage and a black box theater.

If you're in Sin City and you find yourself craving activities of genuine artistic merit, then you can always seek out the Las Vegas Little Theatre. On second thought, stick to boobs.

221. THE RAT PACK

To this day, there have never been bigger swingin' dicks in Vegas than Frank Sinatra, Dean Martin, Sammy Davis Jr., and the other members of the Rat Pack. These guys didn't just play all night, doing whatever they felt like—they helped elect presidents. When Senator John Kennedy took in their show at the Sands in 1960, his street cred went up dramatically.

The Rat Pack may be gone—hell, the Sands is gone, replaced by the Venetian—but the shadow of the Rat Pack continues to loom large in Sin

City. For one thing, you'll see actors portraying them, roaming around the Venetian. For another, there have been, what, three movies now based on *Ocean's 11*, the quintessential Rat Pack film, from 1960.

> ❝ WE AIN'T FIGURED OUT OURSELVES WHAT THE HELL WE DO UP HERE, BUT IT'S FUN, BABY. ❞
>
> —Frank Sinatra

The original *Ocean's 11* was a movie made cool only by the entire cast's *who-gives-a-shit* attitude. But who else would have been given permission by major Strip properties to showcase the theft of casino proceeds? Just the Rat Pack, baby.

222. ELVIS: THE KING OF VEGAS—AND EVERYTHING ELSE

Before he became a grotesquely overweight, hyper-sweaty self-parody and died in his Graceland bathroom, Elvis Presley *was* Las Vegas. To this day, his legions of impersonators are marrying senseless drunk couples. Grotesquely overweight—oops, make that overpriced—Cirque du Soleil puts on an Elvis show. And impersonators wonder the streets like sequined zombies.

> ❝ I'VE NEVER GOTTEN OVER WHAT THEY CALL STAGE FRIGHT. I GO THROUGH IT EVERY SHOW. ❞
>
> —Elvis Presley

The first time Elvis played Sin City, he bombed. In 1956, folks just weren't ready for the "atomic-powered singer." They were used to fancy revues put on by has-beens. It wasn't until Elvis himself became a has-been that he managed to find a huge Las Vegas fan base.

Elvis first played the International (now the Las Vegas Hilton) on July 26, 1969. He was a smash. Entertainers had been money losers for casinos but made up for the black ink by luring suckers to the casino floor. Elvis marked the first time an entertainer *made* money for a casino. So, we have the King to thank for the inflated prices charged by everyone from Céline Dion to Paul Anka. Thanks, Elvis! *Thangya verruh much!*

223. PENN AND TELLER

One guy's a loudmouth. One guy never speaks. Together, they're a weird combination of magic and comic edginess. They have a TV show on Showtime called *Bullshit!* And they've become as woven into the fabric of Las Vegas as illegal hookers.

Penn (Jillette) and (Raymond Joseph) Teller (Churchman) first teamed up in 1975. Since 2001, they've been headliners at the Rio Hotel and Casino. Penn is a freakishly tall, very loud guy who acts as the duo's emcee. Teller, like Harpo Marx, remains silent onstage and is a skilled magician.

> SURE, WE'RE SMUG, SELF-RIGHTEOUS, POMPOUS, AND SELF-IMPORTANT ASSHOLES, BUT DAMN IT, WE'RE RIGHT!
>
> —Penn

Typical tricks often involve putting Teller in what appears to be mortal danger. Sometimes he's drowned, sometimes he's descended over spikes, sometimes he swings over bear traps.

For some reason, they just seem to belong in a place like Las Vegas. Maybe it's their appearance of recklessness. Maybe it's their appearance of insouciance. Or maybe their show makes people feel they can survive any odds, even the bullshit ones offered in the casino.

224. SIEGFRIED AND ROY

They were *so* fabulous, and if you never saw them, then you never will. The magic-and-white-tiger duo gave their last show in 2009, some six years after Roy nearly got killed by one of his tigers.

Siegfried (Fischbacher) and Roy (Horn) met in 1959 on a cruise ship and quickly joined forces. Siegfried is a magician, and Roy works with exotic animals. They became headliners at The Mirage Hotel and Casino in 1990. With cheap seats costing in the low six figures, it's no surprise that Siegfried and Roy once were the ninth-highest-paid celebrities in the United States. The show ended abruptly on October 3, 2003. During a performance, Roy was attacked by a white tiger named Montecore.

> IN ALL OF US THERE IS AN ILLUSIVE MELODY WHICH WHEN HEARD AND FOLLOWED LEADS US TO THE FULFILLMENT OF OUR FONDEST DREAMS.
>
> —Siegfried or Roy or both

In 2009, the couple—and Montecore—reunited for Siegfried and Roy's final show, leaving fans of obscenely high-priced Las Vegas shows one less venue at which to throw away their money.

225. COOK E. JARR AND THE KRUMS

Lounge lizards curl up and die on the scorching Vegas streets in the presence of Mr. Cook E. Jarr because he is the myth, the mullet, the *man*. He would be laughed out of venues in most cities, but in Sin City, Jarr has been booty-shakin', gold-chain wearin', and furiously emotin' for decades. No one—maybe not even Jarr himself—knows what his real name is. His age? Who knows. He's ageless.

This human jukebox stays current by learning every popular song the moment it hits the charts. Within days, he'll be at his regular Harrah's Hotel and Casino gig, parroting those hits in his inimitable style.

> " YOU'RE ON THE LAS VEGAS STRIP, BABY, DANCING YOUR BOOTY OFF TONIGHT! PARTY ON THE LAS VEGAS STRIP WITH COOK E. JARR! "
>
> —Cook E. Jarr

Jarr first arrived in Las Vegas in the early 1970s, with his band, The Krums. But in those days, folks were into Sinatra. Jarr was a swinger, all right, but more in the R & B mode. He ran to Atlantic City, returned to Vegas for a limited engagement in 1982, and has been groovin' in Sin City ever since.

Mr. Cook E. Jarr: Long may your freak flag fly!

226. THE RISE AND FALL OF HOME COOKIN'

Sin City's own version of Tower of Power came just short of hitting the big, big time.

Home Cookin' was a horn-heavy funk band formed in the late 1980s by Frank Klepacki and others. The group's first album—*Mmm, Mmm, Mmm*—was released in 1997, and some of its songs received national airplay. "Soul Space Express," for example, was used for a video game and was featured in the short-lived series, *Cupid*.

In Las Vegas itself, Home Cookin' ruled the local scene for most of its existence. After all, despite its status as "the entertainment capital of the world," the city has spawned very little homegrown talent. That has changed lately, thanks to such groups as Panic at the Disco (see #227) and The Killers (see #228), but for many, many years the Las Vegas music scene sucked. No really: it *sucked*.

Home Cookin' chose to create its own label to release its next album. Two of the group's members left, and 2000's *Pink in the Middle* didn't meet with breakout success. The group called it quits.

> **COMING TO A VIDEO GAME NEAR YOU**
> Home Cookin' founder Frank Klepacki has gone on to success as a composer of video game music. He is best known for scoring the Command and Conquer series.

227. PANIC AT THE DISCO

Not all the performers in Las Vegas specialize in shitty covers of songs that haven't been hits since Phil Spector was known more for his music than for being a coke-sniffing, gun-toting, b-movie-starlet-murdering weirdo.

Case in point: Panic! at the Disco.

The group was formed in 2004 by childhood friends and Palo Verde High School (Las Vegas) alums, Ryan Ross and Spencer Smith. Like many bands, the group has had its share of back-stabbing drama, so the group now is comprised of Smith and singer/keyboardist Brendon Urie.

> 66 HEY, I'LL BE A PRETTY BOY FOR MONEY. 99
>
> —Brendon Urie

The group's first album, *A Fever You Can't Sweat Out*, rose to number thirteen on the Billboard music charts thanks to such songs as "But It's Better if You Do" and the Vegas-appropriate "I Write Sins Not Tragedies."

Panic at the Disco's second album, *Pretty. Odd.*, not only featured the loss of the exclamation point after "Panic" but also was a big hit, selling more than a million copies and rising nearly to the top of the charts.

Not bad for a group that started out as a Blink 182 cover band!

228. THE KILLERS REALLY ARE FROM LAS VEGAS

If you always thought The Killers were a British band, then don't feel *too* stupid. They took their name from a bass-drum image in a New Order video. Their sound is vaguely Brit-pop. And they first hit it big in the UK.

The truth is, this fifteen-million-album-selling band is from Sin City, a town known for gambling, drag shows, and pawned wedding rings . . . but not so much for pop/rock music.

And that's sort of why the group formed in the first place. Leader Brandon Flowers was abandoned by his previous band, which set off for greener pastures in California. He formed a new group, whose demo tape made it to England (after being rejected by pretty much everyone in the U.S.). The group was signed; its first album, *Hot Fuss*, was a big hit, and . . . there you have it: The most successful band ever to come out of Vegas.

> AS I GET OLDER, I HAVE THIS DESIRE TO REPRESENT LAS VEGAS.
>
> —Brandon Flowers

Rumors that they will be the backing band on Wayne Newton's next CD are, apparently, unfounded. Rumors that Flowers is making a solo record are, apparently, not. *Flamingo* (tentative title) will probably be out by the time you read this.

229. VEGAS GOES GONZO: HUNTER S. THOMPSON

Gonzo journalist Hunter S. Thompson may not have been from Sin City, but he certainly put Las Vegas on the literary map with his 1972 *roman a clef*, *Fear and Loathing in Las Vegas*. (A *roman a clef* is a novel based on real-life events.)

Purporting to be a nonfiction "savage journey into the heart of the American Dream," *Fear and Loathing* is, basically, a very (amusingly and/or shockingly) distorted version of what happened to Thompson and a friend when Thompson was in town to cover a car race and, later, a policeman's convention.

> **I HATE TO ADVOCATE DRUGS, ALCOHOL, VIOLENCE, OR INSANITY TO ANYONE, BUT THEY'VE ALWAYS WORKED FOR ME.**
>
> —Hunter S. Thompson

Through Thompson's lysergically-altered view, the already-a-freak-show-when-sober Las Vegas becomes a terrifying zone of the insane, half-crazed, or just-run-of-the-mill-seriously-twisted people and events that take place regularly in the world's favorite desert playground.

Thompson's book was made into a movie in 1998, but ignore the forgettable film. Go for the actual book.

230. THE GOLDEN GLAM BOY OF VEGAS

Not everyone in Las Vegas is an overweight, buffet-slurping man or woman of advanced middle age, though you'd be forgiven for thinking so. Las Vegas also gave birth to a world-class athlete.

> **BEING NUMBER TWO SUCKS.**
>
> —Andre Agassi

Andre Agassi, who retired in 2006, is a former world number one tennis champion. He's the *only* male tennis player to win what's called a Career Golden Slam in singles tennis. That means he not only won all of the sport's Grand Slam titles (only five other men have done *that*) but also won a gold medal at the Olympics.

In his early years, Agassi looked like he would be remembered more for his swagg than for his playing ability. He wore his hair extremely long and, for a time, boycotted Wimbledon because he did not like its emphasis on wearing tennis whites at the expense of donning other, brighter colors.

After winning his first Grand Slam (at Wimbledon, no less) in 1992, Agassi was on his way. Prior to retirement, Agassi found time to marry, then divorce, Brooke Shields and then to marry fellow Career Golden Slam winner, Steffi Graf.

231. OUR OWN NATIVE QUEEN OF PORN

Where does the reigning "Queen of Porn" hail from? Now, don't tax that little brain of yours too much. That's right! Sin City!

Jenna Jameson (born Jenna Massoli) is arguably the world's best-known porn actress. Perhaps even she doesn't even know how many porn videos she's been in since first gaining attention in 1994's *Up and Cummers 10* and *Up and Cummers 11*.

> **I'M GOOD AT A LOT OF THINGS—SEX BEING ONE OF THEM—SO I THINK I'VE CERTAINLY SUCCEEDED AT THAT.**
>
> —Jenna Jameson

The daughter of a Las Vegas policeman and a Las Vegas showgirl couldn't be a showgirl herself because of her diminutive stature. After a stint at Disneyland, she began to dance at Las Vegas strip clubs, though underage. One (possibly true, possibly not) story is that she couldn't get a job at Crazy Horse Too until she pried off her braces with pliers.

Jameson went on to a lucrative career in the pornographic arts. She rakes in money, hand over intimate body part. Her porn company, Club-Jenna, is worth tens of millions of dollars.

Nowadays, she appears mostly to be busy fighting an alleged Oxy-Contin addiction and being allegedly beaten by her husband, UFC champion, Tito Ortiz.

232. CAPTAIN QUIRK: BARRY ZITO

Since he's known for being weird, Las Vegas probably doesn't want you to know that it's the hometown of major league baseball pitcher Barry Zito. Sure, Zito is good. He won the American League Cy Young Award in 2002. He's made three all-star teams. When he left the Athletics for the Giants in 2007, his contract was worth $126 million.

But he's better known for being so weird that his nicknames are Planet Zito and Captain Quirk.

On the field, he has been known to strike yoga poses and meditate before games. He credited a mysterious "universal life force" with helping him make a mid-season turnaround. He used to have blue hair.

Off the field, Zito has a tendency to buy his signed baseball cards on eBay, rather than just buying blank cards and autographing them himself. He said he picked the number "75" for his Giants uniform because the "seven" and the "five" made a good shelf for holding up his name.

> I REFUSE TO BE MOLDED INTO SOME STEREOTYPICAL BALLPLAYER THAT HAS NO INTERESTS, REALLY, NO LIFE, NO DEPTH, NO INTELLIGENCE.
>
> —Barry Zito

233. DIVA LAS VEGAS

Céline Dion has come a long way from rural Charlemagne in the province of Quebec to reign as the Queen Diva of Vegas. The youngest of fourteen children in a highly musical family, Céline was discovered at age twelve—by the much older man she later married. From 2002 until 2007, Dion landed a five-year run, more than 700 sold-out shows, that warranted a completely new theatre. All the backdrops—including Times Square, a train station and a Florentine campo—were broadcast on a giant $6 million LED screen. Other "props" included flying pianos and violins above Céline's head, leaping flames, and a revolving moon on a background screen. The show also had a wordless Romeo and Juliet interlude, a tree that would bloom onstage, a flying orchestra, and a baby dressed entirely in white to represent the moon.

Now that she's expecting twins and anxious to have a settled life again, Dion will return to Las Vegas in 2011 for a three-year residency, once again at the Colosseum at Caesar's Palace.

234. SHOW TOPPERS

After Céline's show closed in 2007, some claimed Las Vegas's talent bookers AEG courted Barbra Streisand, one of very few performers to win a Grammy, an Oscar, a Tony, and an Emmy, plus selling more than 140 million discs in an unbroken forty-seven-year career. Supposedly they offered $100 million for a three-year run, to which Barbra politely declined. AEG Live Las Vegas Vice President John Nelson poo-poohed the report, noting that he thought Neil Diamond would be a great catch.

> **I THINK IT'S THE FIRST THEATER CONSTRUCTED JUST FOR SINGERS . . . AND REALLY, I'M SINGING FOR ONLY AN HOUR AND A HALF. THEY DON'T WANT THE SHOW TO EXCEED THAT BECAUSE THEY WANT PEOPLE TO GO BACK AND LOSE MONEY.**
>
> —Céline Dion

235. DIVA DIGS

In typical *divaesque* style, Céline required certain, shall we say, accommodations to best preserve her voice. The Colosseum designated a private elevator for her use, a below-stage, eight-room suite exclusively for her family, and a $2 million atmospheric bubble that kept the onstage humidity at 55 percent. Her dressing room was essentially an entire home under Caesars Palace, with a living room, kitchen, office, and a garage that held a blue Ferrari, a Father's Day present from Céline to René Angélil, her husband/manager. Although she had toned down her costumes and chopped off her long hair, Dion arrived at the first post-show press conference sporting a glittering silver cape and feather boa. The casino had Céline roulette and blackjack tables where winners received gambling chips with the singer's face imprinted on them.

> WE DON'T LIVE IN A CASINO, AND I AM NOT GOING TO CHANGE DIAPERS ON A CRAPS TABLE.
>
> —Céline Dion

CÉLINE BY THE NUMBERS

Of course, her show was a remarkable success. Consider these numbers:

- ♠ $747 million: Céline's earnings in the last decade
- ♠ $400 million: The amount Dion's Vegas show grossed
- ♠ $100 million, plus half of profits: Amount Dion earned
- ♠ $95 million: The amount Caesars spent for the 4,000-seat theater built specially for Dion
- ♠ 3 million: Number of people who caught Dion's Las Vegas show

236. THE ULTIMATE IN FABULOSITY

Cher, the cherished icon of pop reinvention, opened her own song-and-dance concert spectacle in May 2008 at the 4,100-seat Colosseum in Las Vegas's Caesars Palace, serving up a visually unbelievable hit parade that entailed elaborate choreography, complex staging, stunning costumes, fourteen dancers, and four aerialists. Cher revealed:

"Our set moves down from the ceiling, in from the sides, up from the floor. We have screens in the foreground, the center and the back. We can change a city into a forest in two seconds. You'll see a different stage for every song."

Her favorite designer, the also legendary Bob Mackie, designed all the costumes, some of which heralded Cher's greatest hits and won their own round of applause when they hit the stage. Cher made her first appearance as a singing hologram amid a shimmering laser pyramid, then later descended from the rafters in an open ski gondola tricked out with an Aztec neon sunburst that she called her "Flying Wallenda, Evel Knievel death-mobile."

> I THINK THAT THE LONGER I LOOK GOOD, THE BETTER GAY MEN FEEL.
> —Cher

237. TURNING DOWN THE KING

One of Cher's biggest regrets is that she turned down an invitation from Elvis Presley to spend a weekend together in Vegas. "I was just too young and frightened at the time," she reported, "and I've regretted it forever."

> YOU'VE PROBABLY NOTICED ALREADY THAT I'M DRESSED LIKE A GROWN-UP . . . I APOLOGIZE TO THE ACADEMY, AND I PROMISE THAT I WILL NEVER DO IT AGAIN.
> —Cher, the night she won her Academy Award for *Moonstruck*

238. VIVA LAS DIVAS

Oddly enough (although not too odd for Vegas) one of the hottest divas in town is the headlining female impersonator, Frank Marino. In his own inimitable Joan Rivers style, Marino hosted the hit show "An Evening at La Cage" for many years. Like all the divas before him, Marino loves donning Bob Mackie gowns and loads of jewelry so was thrilled to headline with a coterie of impersonators for his latest show, "Divas Las Vegas." Among the divas they've chosen are Cher, Diana Ross, Liza Minneli, Madonna, Bette Midler, Shirley Bassey, Dolly Parton, Donna Summer, Wynonna Judd, and newcomers Lady Gaga, Beyoncé, Britney Spears. The show also features what Marino describes as six "hunky" male dancers.

> **TEFLON DIVA**
>
> Female impersonator Frank Marino won accolades as the longest running headliner on the Strip, starring for twenty-five years in "An Evening at La Cage" at the Riveria.

" I HAVE SEVENTEEN NEW BOB MACKIE GOWNS. IN HELPING TO DESIGN THEM, I KEPT WITH MY MOTTO, 'TOO MUCH IS JUST ENOUGH.' "

—Frank Marino

239. THE DIVINE MISS M

Bette Midler's "The Show Must Go On" featured her usual backup trio, long known as the Harlettes, and twenty leggy chorines who in turn backed them up. "The best thing is," Midler quipped onstage, "not one of them is a French-Canadian circus performer!" She was referring, of course, to the ubiquity of the Cirque du Soleil brand in the city, and maybe a tad to her predecessor Céline. For her extravaganza, Bette reached back in her past to include characters Delores DeLago, the wheelchair-riding mermaid with the tacky lounge act, and Soph, the naughty joke mistress modeled on Sophie Tucker, who she *Vegasized* by having her don a head-dress "half the size of Tennessee."

> ❝ VEGAS—THE ONLY TOWN THAT COULD TEACH KRAFT SOMETHING ABOUT CHEESE. ❞
>
> —Bette Midler

240. THERE'S SOMETHING IN THE AIR

"Miss Dion"—as Bette Midler calls Céline—warned The Divine Miss M (Bette's alter-ego dating back to the 1970s) about the lack of humidification and the horrors that can hamper a singer's voice in the desert. "They used to think it was because of the way they used to clean the carpets . . . put powder down and vacuum it up," Midler said, noting the legendary tale that way back in 1981, after agreeing to a then-Strip record of $350,000 for one week at the Riviera, Dolly Parton got Vegas Throat on her first night and didn't set foot onstage the rest of the week. Doctors now say "Vegas Throat" is caused by the low desert humidity and dust particles in the air combining to mimic the effects of an allergy attack.

SAYING IT WITH FLOWERS

On opening night of "The Show Girl Must Go On," Bette Midler received flowers and gifts aplenty. Among them: white roses from Goldie Hawn, a tasteful arrangement from Oprah, a three-foot-long reclining white tiger from Siegfried and Roy, and a huge, fragrant arrangement featuring a Styrofoam mannequin head with a tall showgirl headdress from the theatre's previous diva: Céline Dion.

" AT FIRST I SAID, 'IT'S NOT ME. IT'S NOT ME.' BUT EVENTUALLY YOU HAVE TO FACE IT. IT IS YOU. THIS IS WHAT YOU DO. YOU LOVE SPARKLES. YOU LOVE SHOWGIRLS. YOU LOVE BOAS AND FEATHERS. YOU LOVE BOOBS. I'M LIKE A MAGPIE. I'M A SUCKER FOR WHATEVER GLITTERS. "

—Bette Midler, on why she finally said "yes" to a Vegas show

241. BETTE'S LOST WAGES

Even though Bette Midler married Martin von Haselberg in Vegas, with a moonlighting Elvis impersonator officiating, she's harbored a grudge dating back more than thirty-five years. She had her first big Vegas gig opening for Johnny Carson at the Sahara, and got less than a rousing ovation. "They just didn't know what to make of me," she'd said back then. "They didn't understand why they had left the gambling tables."

" ELTON, CHER, ME? DOES IT GET ANY GAYER? "

—Bette Midler

242. UNLUCKY LADY

Just before her second marriage failed and she was left nearly bankrupt, Debbie Reynolds purchased thousands of items from the great MGM auction of 1970—including Judy Garland's 'Dorothy' dress from *The Wizard of Oz*, Marilyn Monroe's 'subway' dress, a Betty Grable bathing suit, and Julie Andrews's jumper and guitar from *The Sound of Music*. Luckily, she had formed a non-profit corporation to preserve her treasures. Unluckily, her husband's finances crumbled, leaving her scrambling to find work.

In 1984, Debbie married her third husband, Richard Hamlett, and together they purchased and renovated the Paddlewheel Hotel in Las Vegas, renaming it the Debbie Reynolds' Hollywood Hotel and Casino. Finally she had a home for her treasured collection of Hollywood props, sets, and costumes. Unluckily, the hotel and casino went belly-up in 1997 and when The Wrestling Federation purchased the hotel and casino at a bankruptcy auction for $10 million, it was far less than the claims against it—once again leaving Debbie to bear the brunt of the bill. Debbie moved her treasures into storage once again. In 2005, she finally opened Debbie's Hollywood Motion Picture museum on Belle Island Resort in Pigeon Forge, Tennessee.

REEL LIFE

The Hollywood Motion Picture Museum contains the largest collection of Hollywood movie memorabilia in the world, including items from almost every academy award-winning film and star from the silent era through the late 1970s. The collection is so extensive that the museum rotates exhibits four times a year, and expects it to take more than thirty years before they complete the first full rotation of the collection.

" I DO TWENTY MINUTES [OF PERFORMING] EVERY TIME THE REFRIG-ERATOR DOOR OPENS AND THE LIGHT COMES ON. "

—Debbie Reynolds

243. ETERNITY IN VEGAS

When they're alive, you can't usually get close to famous folks. Unless you're paparazzi. Or a stalker. Or just lucky. But there are some celebs you can visit in Las Vegas any time.

Arguably the most famous dead celebrity in Las Vegas is Redd Foxx. The star of *Sanford and Son* went to his final reward in October 1991. He is buried in the Palm Valley View Memorial Park.

Charles L. "Sonny" Liston died somewhere around December 30, 1970. When he was found by his wife the first week of January 1971, the former heavyweight boxing champion had been dead for a few days. Officially, he died of natural causes, but many suspect foul play. He is buried in Paradise Memorial Gardens.

GROUND CONTROL TO COLONEL TOM

Some sources say that Colonel Tom Parker, Elvis Presley's controversial manager, is buried in Las Vegas. Other sources say he isn't. Jinkies! We have a mystery!

The first "big name" to give Frank Sinatra his start also can be found in Sin City . . . well, sort of. Bandleader Harry James died in 1983, nine days after giving his final concert, in Las Vegas. He is buried in Bunker Eden Vale Memorial Park. Sinatra gave his eulogy.

244. HAUNTED CASINOS

Las Vegas tries to pretend death doesn't exist. People get plastic surgery to look young. Buildings get imploded before the graffiti in their bathrooms can dry. Nonetheless, the dead make themselves known in Sin City.

The Flamingo Las Vegas, for example, is said to be haunted by the ghost of its founding father, Benjamin "Bugsy" Siegel (see #145). When he was in town, Siegel stayed in a special penthouse suite. After his death, the suite was removed, but supposedly Siegel sometimes appears in the area where it used to be.

The Luxor is said to be haunted by one or both of the two construction workers who died in 1992 during construction of the pyramid-shaped property (see #178). Some wackos believe the spot is haunted because of its shape. Pyramids are supposed to be fraught with all kinds of special paranormal power . . . *yadda yadda yadda.*

> **GHOSTS ON DISPLAY**
> Haunted Vegas Tours offers guided tours of these, and other, "haunted" spots in Sin City: *www.hauntedvegastours.com.*

Bally's is said to be haunted because it was the site of a fire that killed eighty-four hotel guests . . . although it was the original MGM Grand then (see #172). People have smelled smoke in some of the upper floors, and the occasional apparition has been sighted.

245. SIN FLICKS

Oddly enough, the first "Las Vegas" movie doesn't focus on gambling, *and* it concerns the transformation of a sinner to a saint. Fortunately, it didn't take long for Vegas films to focus on gambling, alcohol and drug addiction, murder, and, of course, sex.

Boulder Dam (1936) is about a guy who accidentally kills his boss with a too-well-connected punch, flees to Las Vegas, gains work on the Boulder—a.k.a. Hoover—Dam project, and learns the error of his ways.

Let's fast forward through a few well-known, though not very good, films: the Rat Pack's *Ocean's 11* (1960) and Elvis's *Viva Las Vegas* (1963). Now we have arrived at the greatest shitty story set in Las Vegas ever told: *Showgirls* (1995).

The story of so-not-sexy Nomi Malone (the supremely untalented Elizabeth Berkley) didn't just bomb at the box office, it destroyed the careers of nearly everyone involved with it, and single-handedly destroyed the NC-17 rating. Not bad for a film about cat-fighting Vegas strippers! Especially one that went on to earn $100 million in DVD rentals and become one of MGM's top 20 all-time bestsellers.

> **YOU CAN'T TOUCH ME, BUT I CAN TOUCH YOU. I'D REALLY LOVE TO TOUCH YOU.**
>
> —Elizabeth Berkley as Nomi Malone in *Showgirls*

246. GO WEST TO LAS VEGAS, YOUNG MAN

Some 6,000 people move to Las Vegas every month—but 2,000 leave. Since the 1990s, the population has grown more than 55 percent.

247. BETTER LUCK NEXT TIME

That's what the tourists who swarm into Las Vegas each year must think—because 80 percent of them are return visitors. The average visitor makes the trip across the desert two times a year (and no matter where you're coming from, you have to cross the desert).

All we can say is: *Viva Las Vegas!*

INDEX

ABOUT THE AUTHORS

Quentin Parker is an experienced journalist and teacher. He is the author of several books, including *101 Things You Didn't Know about Casino Gambling, His/Hers, Red State/Blue State,* and *101 Things You Didn't Know about Judas.* He lives in North Carolina.

Paula Munier is a veteran writer, editor, and publishing executive. The founding editor of *Las Vegas Weekly,* she's also the author of several books, including *Fixing Freddie, Hot Flash Haiku, Yes, You Can!,* and *101 Things You—and John McCain—Didn't Know about Sarah Palin.* She lives in Boston and Las Vegas.

Susan Reynolds has authored numerous books, including *The Everything® Enneagram Book* and *Change Your Shoes, Change Your Life.* She is the creator and editor of Adams Media's My Hero series, which includes *My Teacher Is My Hero* (2008), *My Mom Is My Hero* (2009), *My Dad Is My Hero* (2009), and *My Dog Is My Hero* (2010). She also edited *Woodstock Revisited: 50 Far Out, Groovy, Peace-Loving, Flashback-Inducing Stories from Those Who Were There.* Ms. Reynolds owns Literary Cottage, a literary consulting firm based in Boston, but she visits Las Vegas frequently for, um, the shopping.